A Pictorial Survey of
LNER
CONSTITUENT
SIGNALLING

A. A. MACLEAN

Oxford Publishing Company

ISBN-86093-146-3

ACKNOWLEDGEMENTS

It would be an impossibility to name all those who have so freely and generously assisted with the compilation of this work, but sincere thanks are expressed to all concerned, and especially to:-

H. G. Smith, Signalling Officer, British Rail, Glasgow.
P. Tatlow, C. Duffell and members of the LNER Study Group.
Nigel Mundy of Rugby.
Dr. John Emslie of Troon.
W. A. C. (Bill) Smith, of Glasgow.
Joseph Rae, and staff of the S. & T. Departments, British Rail, Glasgow and York.
Public Relations Officers of Eastern and Scottish Regions, British Rail.
The National Railway Museum, York.
Scottish Record Office, Edinburgh
Mitchell Library, Glasgow.
Jack Waldock of Hertford.
R. M. Casserley, Berkhamstead.
J. E. Hay of Auchencrow, Berwickshire.
Area Managers and Staff of Eastern and Scottish Region, British Rail.
Ian Scrimgeour, Canada.
P. J. Kelley, British Railways Board.
R. Preston, C. T. Goode, John Watling, Tony Waterfall, Ray Montgomery and others whose names appear in the photographic captions.

BIBLIOGRAPHY

LNER Magazine, 1927-1947
North Eastern & Scottish Magazine, 1923 - 1926
British Railways Magazine
Rule Books of the LNER constituents
Appendices to Rule Books
LNER Civil Engineers Department Minutes
Signalling Layout Plans (Various)
Mechanical Railway Signalling (Rayner Wilson)
Power Railway Signalling (Rayner Wilson)
Railway Magazine
Railway Engineer
Railway Gazette
Modern Railway Signalling (Tweedie & Lascelles)
Institute of Civil Engineers Journals
Institute of Railway Signal Engineers Journals
Signalling Firms Leaflets and Catalogues
'By Rail to Victory' published by the LNER Company
'Great Central' (George Dow) published by Ian Allan Ltd.
LNER official publications

Printed in Great Britain by:
Netherwood Dalton & Co. Ltd., Huddersfield, Yorks.
Typesetting by Aquarius Typsetting Services, New Milton, Hants.

Published by:
Oxford Publishing Co.,
Link House,
West Street, POOLE,
Dorset

Introduction

The study of railway signalling is fascinating by its complexity. The development of the hardware started with the contractors, who, in many cases, were the people who actually built the line. Later, specialized signalling firms emerged and a number of railway companies adopted the products of these firms as their own standard with others following a more parochial approach and designing and making material to their requirements. A third group followed a compromise course and used their own items in conjunction with those from contractors. With the passage of time, many smaller railway companies, often only operating a few miles of track, merged, or were taken over by larger lines and newer standards evolved. Conversely, larger railways adopted the more local approach, especially in items such as signal boxes, often blending with station styles or the immediate environment as part of developing an 'image' for new works and for major extensions. Junctions between railway companies were often responsible for the appearance of 'foreign' equipment and designs, when the existing railway company insisted that the incomer made all the arrangements and supplied materials such as signals, signal boxes, block instruments, etc.

Signalling tended to be less parochial in its development than rolling stock, and also enjoyed greater longevity, with equipment replacements often being to the same pattern as the original, and in this context, a detailed chronology of evolution, even terminating at the calendar date of 1st January 1923, when the constituent lines that formed the London & North Eastern Railway lost their identity, would be cumbersome.

In this work, it is not the intention to produce a definitive work on the practices of the companies which formed the LNER, but to endeavour to give an appreciation to those whose interest in signalling is, perhaps, eclipsed by other features of railways. Where possible, the presentation is in chronological order, and the whole is sub-divided into smaller more definitive sections, each dealing with a particular aspect of the signalling world, in an endeavour to effect clarification.

Where it has been found to be of advantage to look outside the basic LNER network of lines to place an item in context, this has been done, but is minimal. Similarly, where the perfunctory adherence to a 'cut off' date of 1st January 1923 would have compromised a development, this has also been overridden.

It may well be noted that a number of the drawings in the book are not dimensioned. This was done as it was felt that the object of the work was to outline systems, rather than adhere to specific items, and if these omissions confuse or irritate, an apology is tendered.

The author freely admits to a predilection for railway matters north of the border, but hopes that a suitable balance has been achieved for all signalling matters on the constituent lines of the London & North Eastern Railway.

A. A. Maclean
Greenock
September 1983

Contents

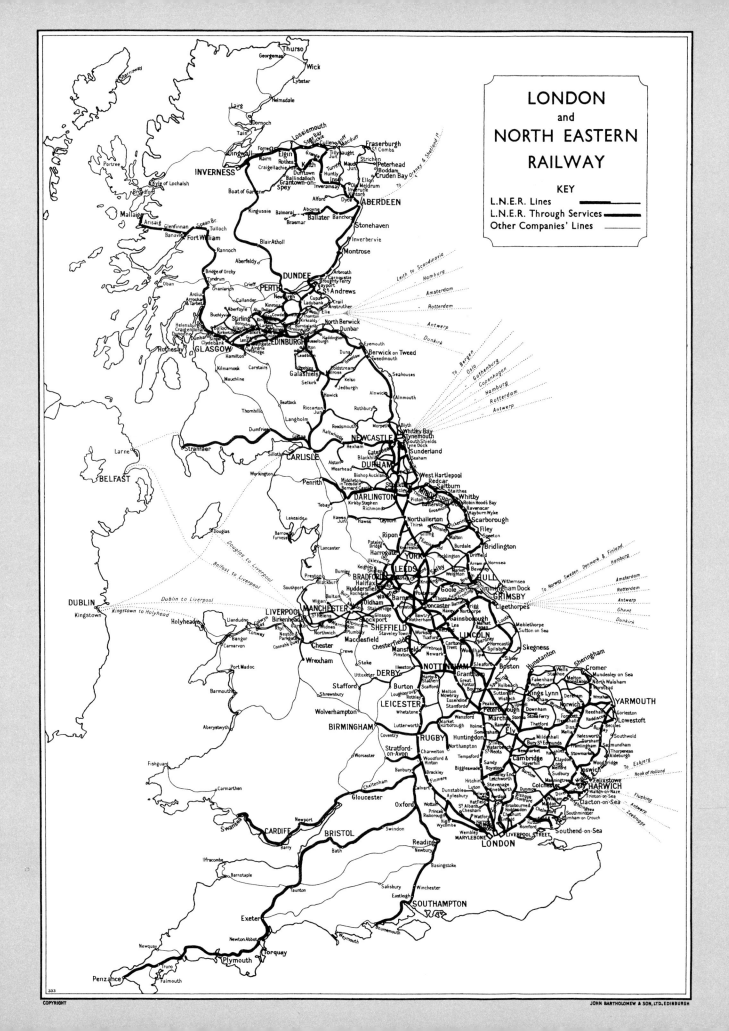

LONDON and NORTH EASTERN RAILWAY

KEY

L.N.E.R. Lines
L.N.E.R. Through Services
Other Companies' Lines

JOHN BARTHOLOMEW & SON, LTD., EDINBURGH

333

Chapter One

Semaphores to Colour Lights

Figure 1: This shows an early Danger signal; the red light being given by hoisting a bucket of red hot coal up a 'gibbet'.

Figure 2: This is an example of a fixed board 'instruction' signal, also from North-East England.

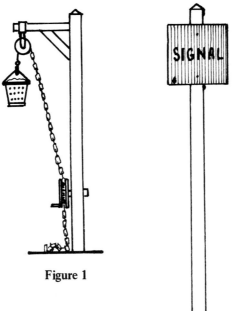

Figure 1

Figure 2

Plate 3: An early Stockton & Darlington signal now in Darlington (North Road) Museum. The triangular board is painted red, the post white with black base. Note the absence of a signal lamp on this example, although some were so fitted with a holding bracket, below the vane. The lamp was double-lensed, with one being red and the other clear. Operation was by hand lever, fitted to the post about 3 ft. from the ground, moving in a horizontal plane.

Author

Plates 1 and 2: These photographs depict current examples of 'fixed board' signals, the lettering being of cast metal screwed to the board. **Plate 1**, at Cambridge, has a rough timber post. **Plate 2**, at Doncaster, being of square section wood. Oil lamps are fitted to both, for location purposes.

Author

Main Line Signalling

The opening of the first steam-operated public railway from Stockton to Darlington, is perhaps a fitting date from which to chronicle this survey of signalling.

The essence of effective signalling is good communication between operating staff, and in those early days this was simply not available. Early signalling devices were usually of a purely local nature to meet an immediate need and variety was legion.

When the first trains ran from Stockton to Darlington, the engine was preceded by a man on horseback bearing aloft a red flag and as his signals, such as they were, applied to the driver, other railway workers, crossing users and trespassers, he can probably be termed as the first railway signalman.

In a more static context, the man who threw live coals in the air or on the ground to denote termination of incline working in Weardale could also be so termed, and although a red signal was produced, the effect on dry vegetation, not to mention staff, who were not perhaps quite so fleet of foot as required, is best left to the imagination. One can also question the validity of this signal in fog, falling snow, bright sunlight or against a sunset.

Neither of the two forms of signalmen above had long innings. The "horseback signalman" fell victim (metaphorically it is hoped) to increases in train speed, while the other was replaced by a more stable and less hazardous system of filling a perforated brazier with red hot coals and hoisting up or lowering from a gibbet-like structure by chain, thereby indicating whether wagons could pass up or down an incline respectively. The gibbet is shown in **Figure 1**.

History records that the signal to a driver to call at a station after dark was given by the placing of a lighted candle in the window of the station house. The absence of such a signal intimated that all was clear to proceed, a principle that was to be followed for many years. 'Fail Safe' was to be of the future.

Initial train operating practice relied on the timetable as the medium to keep trains apart. At junctions, where they existed, trains simply awaited their turn, or came to a stand before the points if there was cause to suspect any out of turn working.

As traffic increased, this elementary method was soon found to be totally inadequate and initially, where regulation was required, this fell to the lot of the railway policemen. The constabularies were located at stations, junctions, level crossings and at such other points where it was considered that their presence was needed to maintain law and order. In addition to these duties, they were enjoined to assist with station working and a logical extension of this was deemed to be train control.

A code of hand signals was devised to facilitate communication with drivers. If a preceding train had not departed a given number of minutes in advance of the next one, the Stop signal was given by extending both arms at right angles to the body. If this time had elapsed, but a second identical period had not, the Caution signal was given by holding one arm above the head. If this second time interval had elapsed, no signals were given. The watch had not attained universal usage, and the policemen were often issued with 'egg timer' type of sandglasses. If no hand signals were given, or the man was simply not there, the driver assumed that the line was clear and proceeded accordingly.

Alternatives to the Stop and Caution hand signals were provided by red and green flags respectively. A white flag was used for Clear. Initial attempts in signalling at night employed fire baskets and torches giving red and white indications, the torch being moved from side to side for 'go on' or 'go back', or up and down for Stop. It was not long before lamps displaced these devices.

It is of interest that in the Rule Book of one early LNER line (there was no standard Rule Book until 1876) the order of signals was white, green and red, in decreasing order of importance — a complete contradiction of later practice.

As the number of trains increased, so did the involvement of policemen with their control and a separate grade of staff evolved, drawn mainly from guards and permanent way staff, specifically to work on signalling equipment. Titles varied according to the line on which they were employed.

Hand and hand held flag or lamp signals developed into fixed, or 'standard' structures, some of which used flags for a short time, although when the flag flew parallel to the rails, or wrapped itself round the support, it defeated its object. Initially, most early 'standard' signals were located at, and worked by staff, at stations and junction points, but there were also places where some form of signal was required, yet it was uneconomic to provide staff. In this case, recourse was made to erecting fixed board type signals, generally a red painted board of various shapes atop a wooden post. The appropriate wording was often endorsed on the board and these signals, as shown in **Figure 2** can be said to exist today as 'whistle' etc. boards as in **Plates 1 & 2**.

The first 'standard' signal to display more than one aspect appeared about 1830, one type being a red triangular board mounted atop a rotating rod, the lower end of which was fitted with a handle about 2 feet 6 inches from the ground moving in a horizontal plane. One of this type has been preserved in Darlington (North Road) Museum and is seen in **Plate 3**. A lamp was fitted for night operations, originally independent of the rod, but was soon fixed to it. It was a single aspect red lens type. Movement of the board to the 'clear' position turned the lamp out of the approaching driver's range of vision. This signal, used on the Stockton & Darlington Railway is shown in **Figure 3**.

A logical development was the use of a lamp with red and clear lenses at right angles to each other. The former showed through a hole in the red board **(Figure 3)** or fitted below **(Figure 4 & Plate 4)** the clear lens being displayed to

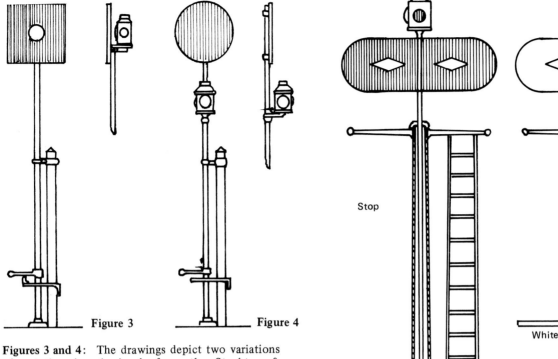

Stop

Clear

Red

White   White

Red

Plan of Vanes

Figure 5

Figures 3 and 4: The drawings depict two variations of rotating board signals from the Stockton & Darlington Railway. In the former, the twin-lensed lamp was arranged to display red through the aperture in the red painted board, the clear lens becoming visible to trainmen when the board rotated through 90 degrees. In **Figure 4**, the lamp was mounted below the board, but indications were identical.

Figure 3

Figure 4

Sectional View

Figure 5 (right): An early Stockton & Darlington Railway 'butterfly' vane signal by Bouch. The provision of the white vanes for 'clear' was an endeavour to provide a positive day indication of the line ahead situation, and it was used on the Darlington to Barnard Castle line about 1860. The controlling wire was attached at the base of the post; the worm being designed to act in a similar manner to 'lifting hinges' with the weight of the arm and lamp restoring to 'danger', but this did not work and conventional balance weights were latterly used.

Plate 4 (left): This is a good example of an early rotating board signal of North Eastern Railway origin at East Anfield, with a double-lensed lamp fixed to a rough wooden post beneath an equally crude board. The lamp is suspended from two supports bolted to the post, there being no base plate.

J. E. Hay

Figure 6 (right): This gives an outline diagram of the 1840 Summerson & Russell twin aspect light signal as was used on the Stockton & Darlington Railway and as viewed from an approaching train. The red board at the top of the post did not rotate and served as a location marker board only, the actual 'stop' or 'proceed with caution' indication being given by the lamp display, as outlined in **Figure 7**. The absence of the lamp, however, gave a similar indication to the trainmen as a normal fixed board signal and was similarly obeyed.

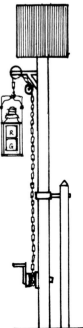

drivers when the board was parallel to the rails. These signals were also used to protect certain road/rail level crossings, some surviving in North-East England in this capacity until recently. **Figure 5** depicts a Bouch signal for the Stockton & Darlington Railway which featured a positive 'day' white indication.

Communication between adjacent signalmen was virtually non existent until the advent of the electric telegraph. One interim device, operated pneumatically, linked the St. Leonards Station of the Edinburgh & Dalkeith Railway with the foot of the adjacent incline, a distance of some 1,200 yards. At the station end of the connecting three quarters of an inch cast-iron tube, a piston was linked to a bell striker, the other end of the tube being equipped with a large pair of bellows. Intimation of the approach of a train was made by a man at the foot of the gradient jumping on the bellows, which seven seconds later rang the station end bell with such force that it was heard a quarter of a mile away.

The first twin aspect 'colour light' signal appeared in 1840. Designed by Summerson and Russell, it was used on the Stockton & Darlington in some locations for about 12 years. The complete signal is shown in **Figure 6**. The actual lamp, shown in **Figure 7**, was 4 feet high, 1 foot wide and 1 foot 10 inches in depth. Internally, it had four separate wicks with reflectors and was equipped for signalling in both directions, having red and green glasses, each ten inches square, on both sides. A metal shutter was provided which could obscure either, or both, coloured glasses. When green was displayed on its own, 'proceed with caution' was indicated, the presence of both colours intimating 'stop'. If one considers the cautionary 'green' as the yellow which was many years later to supplant it, the 'stop' indication was the same as that of a double armed semaphore signal of the 20th Century.

'Time Interval Working' generally dictated that a signal should be placed to Danger after the passage of a train for some five minutes (although the actual time was laid down according to local requirements), then moved to Clear until the next train passed. When the intermediate Caution was introduced, this was displayed for the same period as Danger, but between that aspect and Clear. The normal signal aspect was Clear.

In 1841, Sir Charles Gregory of the London & Croydon Railway introduced to British railways the semaphore signal, based on Admirality signals of the late 18th Century. Simple in concept, the signal arm moved downward through a quarter circle. When horizontal, it meant Stop, when lowered through 45 degrees, Caution, and in the Clear position, the arm fell into a slot in the post. A triple-lensed lamp was mounted on the approach side of the signal post and was linked to the arm-operating mechanism.

Unfortunately, railway engineers of the day did not fully appreciate the significance of this signal. It must be borne in mind, however, that on early railways, signals work, if done at all, was undertaken by the constructing contractor, the normal specification being that it met with the approval of the Directors of the Line, and after 1840, the Board of Trade Inspectorate.

The first detonators were introduced in 1841 by Mr. E. A. Cowper. They were composed of a thin metal casing, two inches in diameter and half an inch deep, with two lead flaps which could be wrapped around a rail to prevent it falling off. A small quantity of gunpowder was placed inside the case which was exploded by the passage of a wheel over it. The idea caught on very rapidly with most railways. Originally designed for working in foggy weather, the device was also used extensively for train protection.

In 'time interval' working, it will be appreciated that when a train left one signal location it was virtually 'lost' until it appeared at the station in advance. During that time, it could slow down or stop with mechanical trouble etc., and there was nothing to stop the man at the signal station in rear admitting a second train under 'clear' signals to the same line provided that the time restrictions had been fulfilled. To meet this problem, some lines, such as the Great Northern and the North British adopted the 'port fire'. A guard was instructed that if his train was running slowly, but going too fast for him to descend and lay detonators, and he saw or heard another train coming up behind him, he was to light and drop a 'port fire', which burned with a red glow for about three minutes. It was also used in fog to supplement detonators.

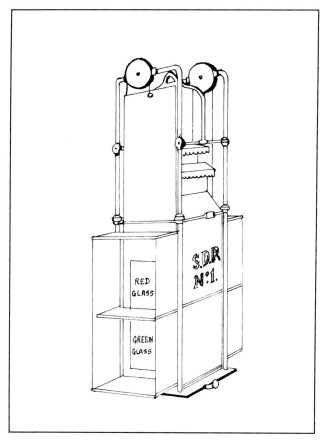

Figure 7: A shutter-operated signal lamp of the Stockton & Darlington Railway, dating from 1840. The 'stop' indication was given by both red and green glass display, but with the red glass obscured by the shutter, leaving only the green glass visible, the indication was 'proceed with caution'. The lamp was used in conjunction with the signal in **Figure 6**.

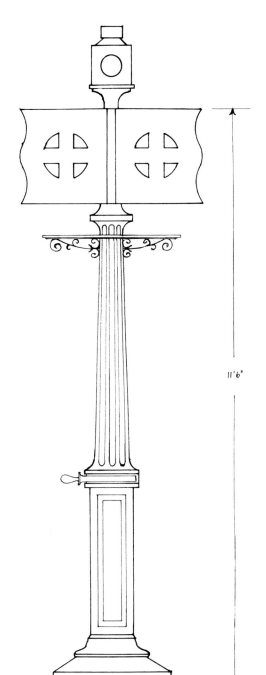

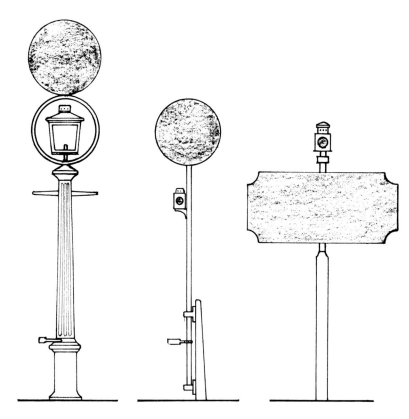

Figure 9: Examples of rotating board signals from (left) Eastern Counties Railway, (centre) Newcastle & Carlisle Railway and (right) North Eastern Railway. In all cases, the vanes were painted red, and a red glass gave the night indication. When the vanes paralleled the running line, a white light was displayed.

Figure 8: A drawing of a typical signal of 'Wood's Patent' type, the decorative iron scroll work and the crossbar shape being varied according to manufacturer and the railway company on which it was used. The oil lit lamp, above the vanes, rotated and in its simplest 'two aspect' mode, had two glazed apertures on adjacent faces, one being fitted with red glass and the other, clear. The red aspect glass paralleled the vanes which were painted red.

Plate 5: Detail photographs of the signal in **Plate 6** showing the vane and decorative scroll ironwork below, on the cast-iron pillar through which the operating rod passed.

Plate 6: Ford Level Crossing on the North British Jedburgh Branch in 1947 before the removal of the old vane signal to York Museum. Note the 'diamond' on the crossing gates and the North British signal lamps, red-lensed, in the centre of each top rail.

LNER

About 1834, Mr. Woods devised the 'standard' signal shown in **Figure 8**, which was made of cast iron, with an internal operating rod manually worked as in previous 'board' types. No positive indication for Clear, other than a lamp, was given. These signals found employment on Scottish lines, such as the Edinburgh & Glasgow (1842) and the North British (1846) almost from the outset. One such signal, albeit minus lamp, still functioned on the Jedburgh Branch at Ford Level Crossing as late as 1947, and is shown in **Plate 6**, with details in **Plates 5 & 7**.

It is impossible to give a pictorial catalogue of all early signal types used on the LNER constituent lines but a few appear in **Figure 9**.

Signalling development placed an increasing burden on staff whose duties were to operate the equipment. The greater the number of points and signals to be worked, the greater the leg work. While certain of their number were relatively well off in their signal houses, or 'homes', those employed at locations where there was a wide area to cover found their work particularly onerous.

In 1847, at Hawick Junction (later Portobello East), near Edinburgh, on the North British Railway, a pointsman named Robert Skelden found that by using cable and a rail chair as balance weight, more than one signal could be operated from his hut. He was reported to the Directors, but far from chastising him, they saw a practical cost saving and endorsed his idea. Skelden submitted details to the Royal Scottish Society of Arts and was awarded a silver medal valued at 'five sovereigns', together with the recognition for inventing the first 'distant' signal in Scotland. No record exists of the actual distances involved, but it may only have been a few yards.

Plate 7: The lower portion of the signal in **Plate 5** showing the operating mechanism. Note the manufacturer's plate on the base and also the strong resemblance to early gas lamp standards.

Author

Undoubtedly the balance weight idea was instrumental in signalling development, wire operation being then in use although on a double wire system, one wire pulling the signal 'on', the other 'clearing' it. Both wires were often coupled to the same lever, a typical example being illustrated in **Figure 10**. In other instances, wires were coupled to other operating mechanisms such as 'stop' signals in rear, thereby making these signals into 'repeaters'. However, there was no indication, other than an easier lever pull, of wire breakages. With non-counterbalanced signals, a false clear could be given due to semaphore arm momentum, this being not quite so serious with rotating 'board' type signals. A simple balance weight is shown in **Plate 8**.

It is perhaps worthwhile at this stage to distinguish between the nomenclature of early signal types.

Figure 10: An early type of signal lever of the Stockton & Darlington Railway, incorporating the balance weight on the handle to restore the signal to Danger when the handle was released. It was used with 'triangle' signals **(Figure 3)**.

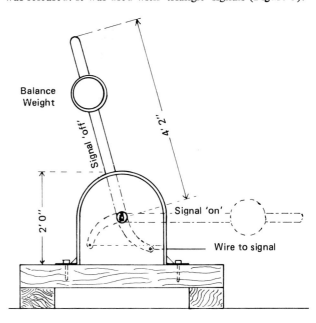

Distant signals evolved from 1834, according to some authorities, because increases in train speeds and traffic density without corresponding increases in braking power, and the locating of signals at stations and junctions, only reduced line capacity. Drivers had to assume that all signals would be adverse and therefore braking had to commence well in advance of the expected signal until they could assure themselves that it was actually Clear. Most railway companies required drivers to come to a stand at such signals and then proceed cautiously. In some ways, this anticipated LNER practice at adverse automatic signals.

'Distance' signals were actually Stop signals, placed about 800 yards in rear of 'station' or 'junction' signals and normally lay 'off', being placed to Danger only if a train was at a stand at the signal in advance, thus avoiding the need for the guard of that train to go back and effect protection. 'Distance' signals were also known as 'Auxiliaries' and it is interesting to note that even after semaphore became widespread, disc, vane, spectacle or other rotating board signals continued to be erected as 'Auxiliaries' under official designation on some lines.

'Station' signals were sometimes rotating boards and on other occasions single arm semaphores placed on the approach to platforms. In some cases, a double arm semaphore with both arms on the same level, but on opposite sides of the post was used. This signal applied to both lines, the respective drivers taking as their signal the arm on the left of the post as they approached. Lamps were, of course, fitted on the approach side of the solid post.

At junctions, and other locations where signals were grouped together and operated from a 'signal house', the normal practice was to mount the posts above the roof of the house to minimize the number of connections between the signal arm and operating mechanism. Because of their location, they became known as 'home' signals, one of the earliest uses of that designation. Several arrangements existed for the positioning of the arms on the post, one being to place the main line arms at the top, the other arms being arranged in decreasing order of importance downwards. An alternative was to make the top arms refer to the line diverging furthest to the left, with arms below arranged in order of divergence towards the right. In other installations, junction signals were mounted on more than one post, but even then, it was not uncommon to find more than one set of arms to each post. Where a number of lines required to be controlled, it was not uncommon to have the signal posts mounted on a gantry structure straddling the rails, with the operator's booth located on the gantry deck, but although this facilitated signal connections, it complicated point linkages. The bracket signal was slow in development and did not really become universal until the 1860s.

It is of interest that although early 'station' semaphores were generally of three position types, at junctions, particularly where facing points were found, only Stop and Caution aspects were used, it being considered essential to remind drivers to exercise caution over the (then) unlocked point blades.

Plate 8: A McKenzie & Holland balance weight on a standard LNER pivot plate at Bishop Auckland.

Author

Early 'standard' signals were usually worked from the base of the actual signal, but with the balance weight development, many of these were converted for remote wire operation, and these became redesignated 'wire' signals.

A further variation in normal practice was found on the lines of the North British and its constituents where at a number of stations only a Caution signal was used. In fact, these signals were termed as Distants although this could merely mean that the signal was 'wire' operated against the 'standard' type. A selection of these signals, all of horizontally rotating type (except the Edinburgh & Leith Railway example which rotated vertically), is included in **Figure 11**.

The Edinburgh & Leith signal, known as the 'spectacle' type because of its resemblance to the sign outside opticians' shops, was also found on the Manchester, Sheffield & Lincolnshire Railway, although in that case, rotation was in the more customary horizontal plane. The lamp unit, which employed candles as illuminant, was raised into its position by windlass, the night indication being given by a single coloured glass slide which moved in a similar manner to single arm semaphores. The slide was removed from the front of the lamp to indicate Clear.

EARLY SCOTTISH DISTANT SIGNALS
(Rotating Board Types)

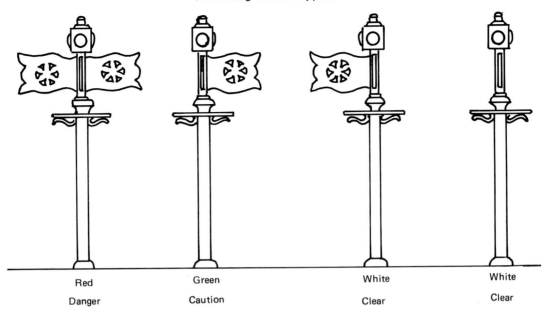

Red	Green	White	White
Danger	Caution	Clear	Clear

NORTH BRITISH (SOUTHERN DIV.) AND EDINBURGH & GLASGOW RAILWAYS

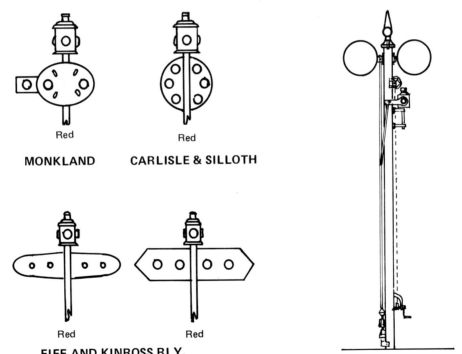

Red — **MONKLAND**

Red — **CARLISLE & SILLOTH**

Red   Red

FIFE AND KINROSS RLY.

EDINBURGH & LEITH

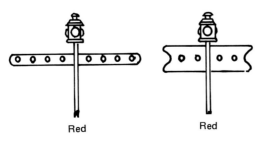

Red   Red

STIRLING & DUNFERMLINE RLY.

Figure 11: All signals rotated in a horizontal plane except the Edinburgh & Leith example, where the lamp moved horizontally, but the vanes moved vertically. Colours shown below each signal give the vane and lamp indication when at 'Danger'. Rotating through 90 degrees made the vanes invisible to oncoming trains, but showed a clear (or 'white') light.

EARLY SEMAPHORE SIGNALS
(All signal arms were painted red)

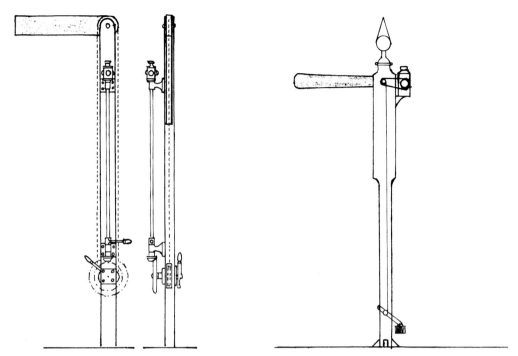

Figure 12: Gregory's original semaphore with the rotating signal lamp gear meshed to the arm mechanism. In the 'Clear' position, the arm fell into the post slot.

Figure 13: Stevens' pattern with fixed lamp and moving spectacle plate, fitted with a single red glass which cleared the lens when the arm fell into the post.

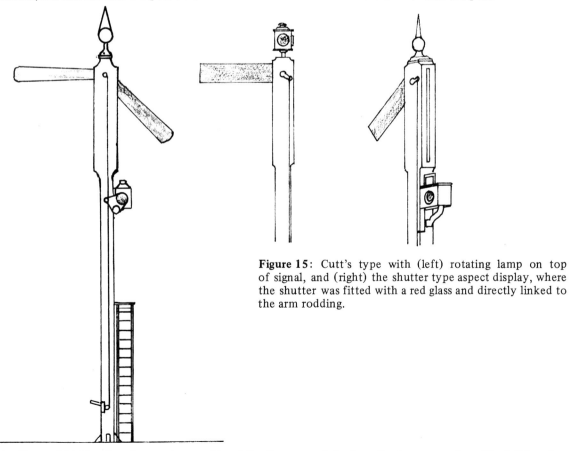

Figure 15: Cutt's type with (left) rotating lamp on top of signal, and (right) the shutter type aspect display, where the shutter was fitted with a red glass and directly linked to the arm rodding.

Figure 14: Stevens' bi-directional semaphore cable of the three aspect display of red, green or clear. The left hand arm is shown in the 'Danger' position, that on the right at 'proceed with caution'.

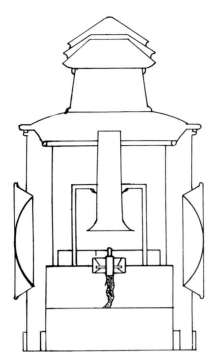

Figure 16: A side section view of an early double-lensed signal lamp with fixed light beam. Non rotating, the lamp was fixed to the post, the different indications being given by independent glazed spectacle plates.

As the semaphore signal gained in popularity, perhaps not unnaturally several variations appeared, although differences were chiefly in minor details such as lamp position and operation. The Eastern Counties Railway used a basically Gregory type as in **Figure 12**, the Scottish lines using Stevens' patterns shown in **Figures 13 & 14**, and the Manchester, Sheffield & Lincolnshire Railway used Cutts pattern, see **Figure 15**. In some Great Northern signals, the arms were perforated, being mounted on an early type of lattice post.

It is interesting to note that the GN used semaphores for Auxiliaries, Distants and Station signals by 1850 and was probably the first major British line to do so. 'Station' signals were of the double armed type, worked by hand levers, one of which survived with an early distant signal lever into the Edwardian era at Edgware, although latterly out of use.

Night indication of semaphore aspects was originally given by lamps with different coloured lenses on each approach side of the signal post. Lamps were of the rotating type, similar in concept to early board signals. Originally independent, they were soon linked to the arm operating apparatus by bevel gears as in **Figure 12**. A double arm signal would therefore have two lamps. About 1848 the practice evolved of mounting the lamp on the side of the post, level with the arm in single armed signals, but below the operating arc of the blade in the double arm type. In the latter case, plain lenses were fitted on opposite sides of the lamp casing, and for both types, red and green aspects were attained by moving appropriately coloured transparent glass across the front of the lens, although in the

'Saxby' type, the colour moved between flame and lens. Cleaning of a Saxby lamp occasionally resulted in the colours being replaced in the wrong order, and this led to the demise of the type which had been used on the MS&L. No glass was provided for the Clear indication, this being given by the normal lens light.

Early signal lamps in use until the 1880s, an example of which is shown in **Figure 16,** were poor performers. The light was said to be equivalent to the contemporary stable lanterns and was contained in a tin box with two holes, four or five inches in diameter fitted with glass 'bullseyes'. No reflectors were fitted normally, the power of the lamp being only four times the power of the naked flame. The presence of coloured spectacles reduced this until it virtually equated with the power of the flame. Light beams were fixed and took no cognizance of line curvature.

One of the first lines to try and balance beam and operating needs was the GN in the provision of specific lamps, duly numbered, for specific signals with a form of pre-set focus. Most other developments were achieved by developing lens shape.

Oil was the normal illuminant, but was not of good quality, and where lamps rotated, the movement was often enough to extinguish the flame. Gas was used, when available, but an alternative to both was the candle, used by the GN in 'Brydones Patent Candle Lamp' for about a decade in the 1850s. In 1857 the MS&L also used this lamp, on GN recommendation, even supplanting gas at some places, apparently on economic grounds.

Access for lamp cleaning and servicing was normally by ladder or spikes hammered into solid posts or bolting cast iron treads to the post, but some lines employed a form of 'windlass' in which the lamp was lowered to ground level, facilitating its flame extinguishment during daylight hours; this was standard GNS and NB practice. Where the arm of this type required maintenance, access was by the unfortunate fitter climbing the lattice, a practice prevalent in the Scottish Region at some locations into the 1950s. The 'windlass' arrangement is illustrated in **Plates 9–12** and also in **Figure 17.**

The universal introduction of the balance weight into semaphore signals greatly increased the range at which they could be operated from a central point and this was readily taken up by the British railway companies. Indeed, the GN had a wire-operated Distant located 1,500 yards from the lever. Unfortunately, unlike today, the normal aspect of signals was Clear and when the wire broke, they therefore reverted to their least restrictive aspect, a practice that caused the Board of Trade disquiet after 1853, although many years passed before their proposals were to bear fruit.

With the exception of the North Eastern, by the mid-1850s the semapahore signal was established on all LNER constituent lines. The North British was introduced to the type in 1851, and such was its spread that by 1855 one of its officers stated that no form of signalling in use at that time could compare with Stevens' semaphore for certainty of action and impossibility of being confounded with other items.

Plate 9: 'Station' signals at Roxburgh Junction in the early 1880s with the adjacent signal house. Each signal is bi-directional and of three aspect type. The signal lamp is in the lowered position clearly showing the large lens size. The coloured glass spectacle plates are above the arms, pivoting downwards so that when the arm was within the slot on the post, the lens was uncovered.

E. Dagg Collection

Plate 10: Details of the 'windlass' arrangement at the base of a Stevens lattice post signal at Musselburgh, with the handle in position. Handles were detachable and normally kept in the lamp room, being suitable for any signal with a windlass.

J. E. Hay

Plate 11: A lamp carrier unit on a North British lattice post signal. The operating chain has broken, the main drum and handle being seen below. A few links remain on the unit.

J. E. Hay

Plate 12: The wheel, mounted within the finial for the windlass arrangement on solid post signals. In lattice post types, the wheel was normally at the top of the lattice.

Author

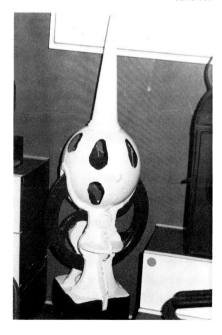

WINDLASS ARRANGEMENT FOR LATTICE POSTS

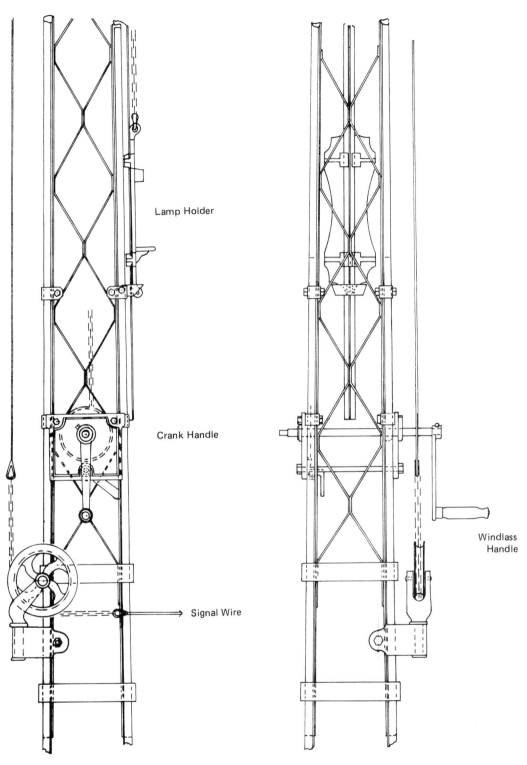

Lamp Holder

Crank Handle

Signal Wire

Windlass
Handle

End elevation of the foot of the post, looking from the direction of an approaching train. The signal lamp is omitted for clarity.

Side elevation from the track centre, with lamp holder in lowered position.

Figure 17

In the early 1850s, some experiments were carried out in automatic signal replacement by trains, one type that found acclaim being the 'Whitworth Automatic Signalling System' which the NB used from 1855 until the early 1860s. Passage of a train depressed a treadle linked to a flat bar of iron which was notched to receive a catch by a transverse bar under the rails. Treadle depression lifted the catch out of the notch, the former then being free to be moved by the signal balance weight which put the signal at its most restrictive aspect until the signalman, in pulling his lever, raised the balance weight and reset the catch. It was, however, unreliable.

Mention has been made of the practice of placing arms for both directions on one post at stations and junctions. Adequate at stations, it offered no protection at junctions unless drivers brought their trains to a stand clear of the pointwork. In conditions of reduced visibility, a driver coming to a stand in a position where he could see the signal might foul the points, or if he stopped clear of the points he might not see the signal. Either way, delays were inevitable.

As the necessity for adquate protection at junctions and realistic braking distances became more acute, grouped signals on one post were replaced by individual signals on separate posts, although where operational requirements or signal sighting permitted, bi-directional arms on common posts or gantries survived.

The adoption of uni-directional signals simplified the practice of spectacle plate location level with the arm, although several arms could be mounted on one post. This was generally required by space restrictions, sighting restrictions or the provision of subsidiary arms. The practice of placing arms and lamps on different levels lasted longest on the GN, a few examples lasting until the late 1970s, as illustrated in **Plate 13**. Examples of multi-arm mounting on single posts are shown in **Plates 14 – 18**.

Although by the mid-1860s most lines operated three position semaphores, development of block systems tended to make the third aspect superfluous as the Caution of the three position system meant the same as the Clear of the two position: in both cases the indication meant the line was clear only to the next signal. Additionally, the Clear aspect of a three position signal meant that the signal arm was hidden in the post. Consequently, signals were gradually altered to have two positions only, the signal lights being red and white for Stop signals, with green and white for Caution or Distant signals. At junctions, red and green gave way to red and white. One of the first lines to standardize on two aspect signals was the Great Eastern.

The 1860s also saw the growing use of the lattice post, introduced by John Stevens and Sons about 1858. These found widespread use on the Scottish lines, which used Stevens as their main contractor for signalling. Elsewhere, the majority of posts continued to be of pitch pine, although gradually differing types of lattice began to be introduced according to the signalling contractor involved.

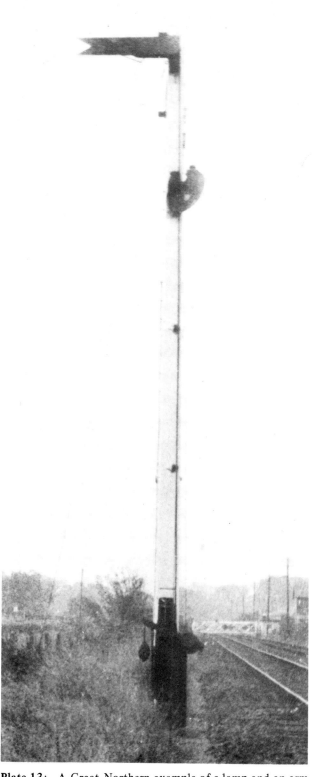

Plate 13: A Great Northern example of a lamp and an arm mounted on different levels, on the Skegness Branch in 1972. The signal post is wooden.

G. Toole

15

Plate 15: Mechanical signal gantry at the west end of Newcastle Central Station, of lattice construction with some 'dolls' equipped for multiple arm and bi-directional signalling. Only a red spectacle glass is provided for each arm, the 'clear' indication being by plain lens display. Three disc signals are mounted on the left hand doll.

Author's Collection

Plate 14: A common post mounting of the North British lower quadrant signals at Heriothill, near Edinburgh. In this instance, both arms were worked from one signal box, the upper being the 'Yard Starter', the lower the 'Outer Home'.

Author

Plate 16: The Railway Signal Company gantry at Edinburgh Waverley (East) dated from 1892 with multiple arm 'dolls' and spectacle plates for all signal arm aspects. The gantry and signal box survived until the resignalling with colour lights in the late 1930s.

Author's Collection

Plate 17: A magnificent gantry of lattice base and wood 'dolls' construction with multiple arm somersault subsidiary signals on the Great Northern Railway's approach to London. Access to the intermediate platform at the top of the latticework is by conventional ladder, as is the right hand 'doll', but access to all the other signal arms and lamps required the climbing of the wood post by the cast-iron steps bolted to the side away from the lamp. Despite the height of the 'dolls', the signal is not accorded the stability of guy ropes or wires, the base of the wood posts being deeply inset into the lattice in compensation.

G. Hemmingway

Plate 18: A fine gantry of predominantly Great Eastern Railway pattern lower quadrant signals on the eastern approaches to Ipswich Station. Note the 'scissors' type of calling on signals and the smaller solid shunting signal on the extreme left hand post. Distant signals, for trains coming towards the photographer, are of the upper quadrant type and are mounted on the same posts as the lower quadrants. Signal dolls are inset into the girder type construction of the signal bridge, but some form of additional strength is given by the signal laddering. Track circuit 'diamonds' are mounted on the appropriate signal 'dolls'.

P. J. Kelley

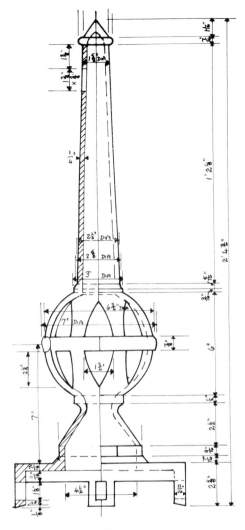

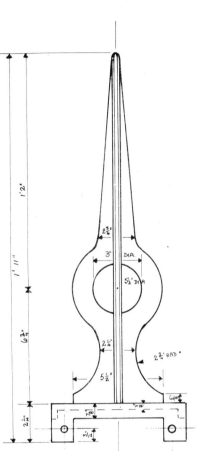

Elevation of the Stevens 'Cruciform' pattern.

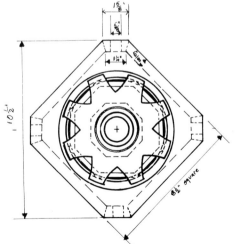

Elevation (top) and plan of the Stevens 'open ball' signal post finial.

Figure 18: Signal Post Finials

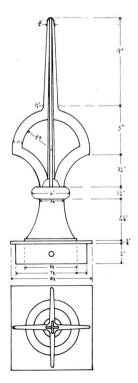

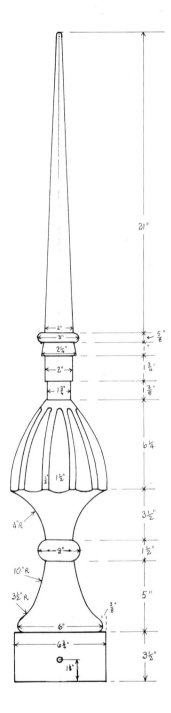

(Above): A signal finial of McKenzie & Holland pattern. A similar one of less height was also produced and generally used, for subsidiary signal arms, on posts or dolls.

(Left): A signal finial of Saxby & Farmer pattern.

Plate 19: A signal finial of the 'ball and spike' type, used inter alia, on the Great Central Railway.

Author

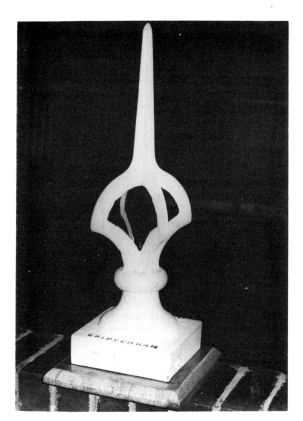

Plate 21: A Saxby & Farmer type signal finial used on the Hull & Barnsley and Great Central Railways.

Author

Plate 20: A McKenzie & Holland type signal finial of a type found on the Great North of Scotland and Great Northern Railways.

Author

Plate 22: An illustration of the Stevens 'open ball' type signal finial on the West Highland section of the North British Railway at Mallaig Junction. The type was also to be found on the Great North of Scotland Railway.

Author

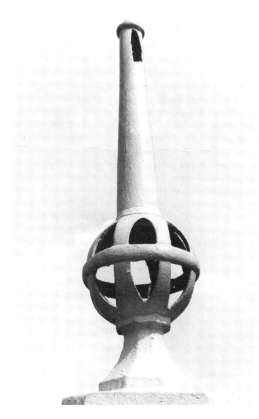

Plate 25: The Humber Graving Dock & Engineering Company plate on the lattice work of a 'down' main line signal, near Cambridge.

Author

Plate 23: The Saxby & Farmer builder's plate on Mallaig Junction 'up' junction signal. Dating from 1895, West Highland signalling was by Saxby & Farmer but the 'house' style of the North British, of 'Stevens' pattern, was retained.

Author

Plate 24: The McKenzie & Holland builder's plate, fitted to a lattice post signal at Tynemouth on the North Eastern Railway.

The grade of Signal Engineer did not make its appearance until the late 1860s, one of the first being appointed to the MS&L in 1870. Many lines, however, used the services of specialized signalling firms, although most had signalling workshops under the jurisdiction of the Civil Engineer. Large contracts for updating existing plant were also contracted out. Specific firms' products began to predominate on each line, and these patterns tended to be specified in tender documents. This gave rise to a certain 'house style' which may have been to one firm's pattern, but made by another, in signal design, although certain items such as lever frames and interlocking were exclusive patterns to specific firms.

A 'trademark' of the signalling contractor was the finial, designs of which were unique, although most lines made them in their own workshops. Stevens' finial was used by the NB and GNS. The McKenzie & Holland (GN and GER) and the Saxby & Farmer (H&B) are shown in **Figure 18**. Variations are shown in **Plates 19—22**. Some firms also affixed their plates to signal posts as in **Plates 23—25**.

The notched end Distant signal arm was introduced in 1872, but it continued to be painted red with a vertical white band, and by night displayed red and white lights (red and green after 1893), the lights being a contributory factor to the Shandon accident of 1895 when a driver took the Home signal as the Distant, having missed the former which was extinguished. Specific deliniation in colour was not introduced until 1916 and will be dealt with later.

Figure 19: Detail drawings of Great Northern Railway somersault signals.

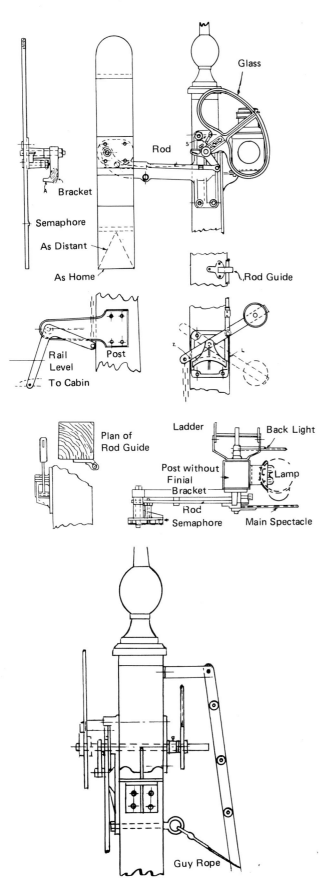

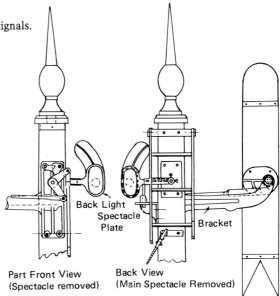

Part Front View (Spectacle removed)

Back View (Main Spectacle Removed)

SIDE VIEW

By 1875, all main line signals of the semaphore type worked in a lower quadrant. However, old two or three position slotted post semaphores (where the arm fell into a slot on the post when Clear) were potentially dangerous. If twin wire control was not operated they were susceptible to being frozen at Clear if that was their 'normal' position. Signals that were not counterbalanced in themselves were also dangerous in that there would be no means of returning to their most restrictive position if any part of the apparatus broke between arm and balance weight (if fitted) or signal box.

All of these hazardous conditions existed at Abbots Ripton on 21st January 1876. The situation was compounded by an inefficient telegraph and the absence of bell codes for trains running away. Although the subsequent accident was mainly due to the failure of the signalman at Woodwalton, in rear of Abbotts Ripton, to lay detonators and exhibit a red hand signal to the 'Flying Scotsman', GNR signalling practices were found wanting.

A provisional patent for a centrally-balanced signal was taken out by a Great Northern Signal Inspector named French, on 22nd September 1877. This operated on the principle of placing a spindle mounted on a bracket casting to the left of the post on the vertical centre line of the arm but above its horizontal centre line so that it was in equilibrium when horizontal, but when vertical had a return effect without counterbalance. Power for the movement of the arm came from a crank on the post activated by a signal down rod. Although no complete specification was lodged, there was a dispute between French and his employers and a financial backer withdrew his support.

The Great Northern was to adopt French's signal, known otherwise as the 'somersault' for most of its signalling operations until it lost its separate identity in 1923. The Lancashire, Derbyshire & East Coast Railway, later part of the Great Central, also used this signal, but it was an expensive type to maintain and most other lines were content to retain the normal spectacle casting and balance weight for signal restoration. The GNR 'somersault' signal is shown in **Figure 19**.

Some indication of the forces normally present in ordinary signals can be gained from the Stevens Pattern illustration in **Figure 20**. Most signal arms were made of cedar, the dimensions varying according to the purpose for which they were employed. A selection of main line arm dimensions is given in **Figure 21**. With wooden arms, it was common to minimize the effects of weathering by binding with metal strips either across the face, or around the edges.

Subsidiary arms varied, both in shape and dimensions, according to their function and similar arms gave different indications on different lines. Appendages such as circles and rings were generally of metal, and a selection of types and purposes is given in **Figure 22**.

Continued on Page 25

Figure 20: A dimensions and force diagram of the weights present in a Stevens' type signal arm, using a former North British type as the example.

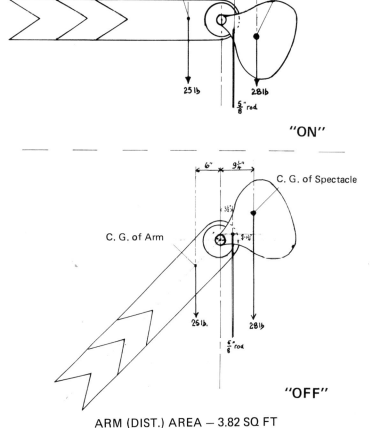

ARM (DIST.) AREA — 3.82 SQ FT

SPECTACLE AREA — 1.77 SQ FT

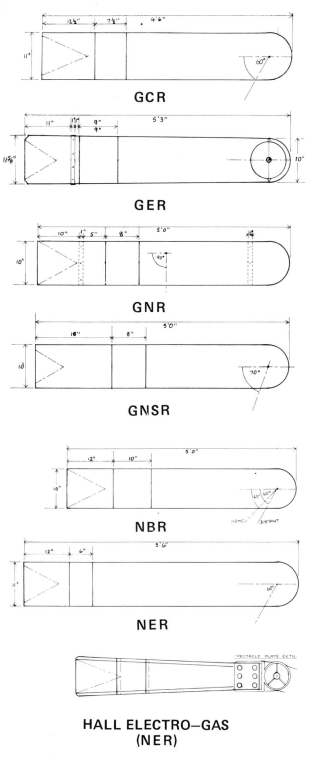

GCR

GER

GNR

GNSR

NBR

NER

HALL ELECTRO—GAS
(NER)

Figure 21: Dimensional sketches of typical signal arms for constituent companies of the LNER.

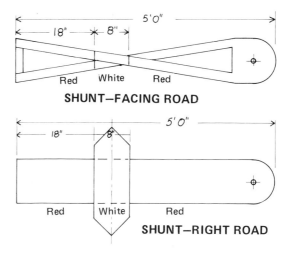

5'0"
18" — 8"

Red   White   Red

SHUNT—FACING ROAD

5'0"
18" — 8"

Red   White   Red

SHUNT—RIGHT ROAD

GN of S

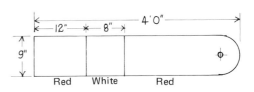

4'0"
12" — 8"
9"

Red   White   Red

GOODS, LOOP OR SLOW LINE

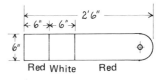

2'6"
6" — 6"
6"

Red White   Red

SHUNT, CALLING ON

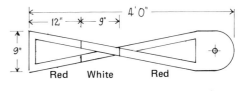

4'0"
12" — 9"
9"

Red   White   Red

SHUNT—FACING ROAD

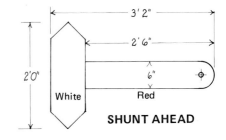

3'2"
2'6"
2'0"   6"

White   Red

SHUNT AHEAD

NORTH BRITISH

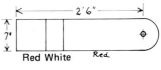

2'6"
7"

Red White   Red

**SHUNT, SIDING OR
CALLING ON ARM**

NER

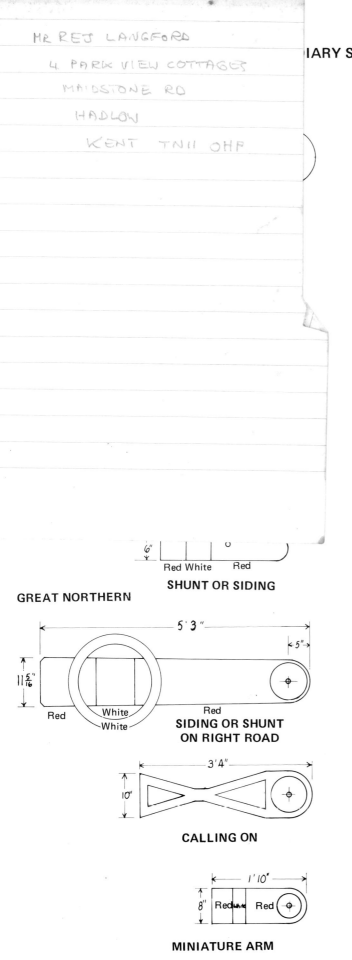

6"

Red White   Red

SHUNT OR SIDING

GREAT NORTHERN

5'3"
5"
11 5/16"

Red   White   Red
         White

**SIDING OR SHUNT
ON RIGHT ROAD**

3'4"
10"

CALLING ON

1'10"
8"   Red White   Red

MINIATURE ARM

GREAT EASTERN

Figure 22

Plate 26: The wire tensioning gear arrangement as used with a McKenzie & Holland frame. The top of the spindle to the gear was 'T' shaped and permitted wire tensioning to take place without a break in the levers as the 'T' head projected above lever level, and was accessible for rotation.

Author

Plate 28: The stirrup type of wire tensioning device used with a Stevens lever frame in Markinch signal box. This is the type shown diagrammatically in **Figure 23** and was fitted adjacent to the frame.

Author

Plate 27: The wheel type of wire tensioning device used in conjunction with a Saxby & Farmer lever frame in Mallaig Junction box. The nearer wheel is devoid of wire, the other having been tensioned.

Author

Plate 29: The lever-mounted wire tensioning stirrups on levers 19 and 21 in a Stevens frame. Note the stirrup between levers 23 and 24 for operating a mechanical detonator placer for the 'up' main line home signal.

Author

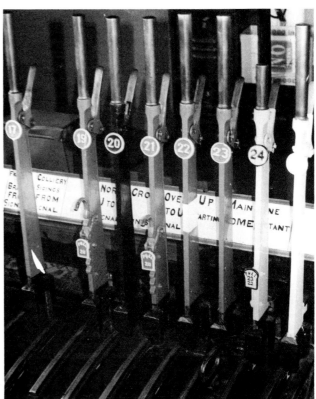

WIRE ADJUSTERS

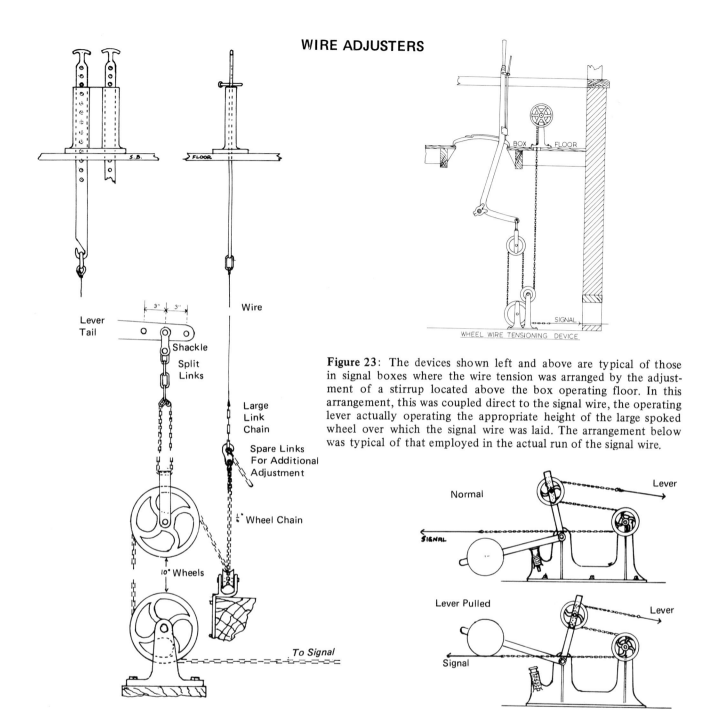

Figure 23: The devices shown left and above are typical of those in signal boxes where the wire tension was arranged by the adjustment of a stirrup located above the box operating floor. In this arrangement, this was coupled direct to the signal wire, the operating lever actually operating the appropriate height of the large spoked wheel over which the signal wire was laid. The arrangement below was typical of that employed in the actual run of the signal wire.

The angle from the horizontal adopted by the arms of two position signals in a 'proceed' position was inconsistent among LNER constituents. Although largely dependent on the signal manufacturer, GE arms fell until the end of the arm was within ten inches of the post. NE and GC arms lay at 60 degrees, GNSR at 70 degrees, NB Homes at 45 degrees and Distants at 60 degrees (angles from horizontal) and GN 'somersault' arms adopted a vertical position, similar to the old three position types, although clear of the post, but in practice all angles were conditioned by tension in the signal wire. The actual position of signal arms that were out of sight of the signal-man was relayed to the box by an electrical 'detector' which gave intimation as to whether the signal arm was 'on', 'off' or 'wrong'. The third indication originated action by the signalman. Some adjusting devices are in **Figure 23**, and in **Plates 26–29**.

Plate 30: A Great Central wooden gantry at Wembley Hill Station, London, with co-acting main line arms.

N. D. Mundy

Plate 31: An 'up' starting signal at Dunfermline Lower with repeating arms of the North British lower quadrant type.

W. A. C. Smith

Plate 32: Tall lattice post signals, at Easter Road, Edinburgh, with suspended repeating arms.

Author

Continuously increasing train speeds requiring adequate braking distances led to many signals being on very tall posts to give a sky background to the arm. Unfortunately, if the lamp was placed level with the arm, the beam decreased in intensity as trains approached. Some lines, such as Great Eastern and Great Northern, divorced arm from lamp. In other circumstances, lamp and arm were duplicated by an identical lamp and arm further down the post, both working from the same signal wire. Illustrations of the Great Northern split level signal are in **Plates 13 & 77**, examples of 'repeating' signals being given in **Plates 30—32**, with wire arrangement in **Plates 33 & 34**.

A classic example of a tall signal, where arm and spectacle plate were on separate levels, could be found in the Distant for the Great Northern '20 Mile Down' signal box, where a 'doll' was provided that was no less than 49 feet tall, a substantial weight to be carried on an ordinary lattice post. When the signal was erected, about 1893, special tackle was hired from London to place the 'doll' in position, and although braced intermediately between bracket and finial, a second bracing strut had to be applied later at a higher level. As illustrated diagrammatically in **Figure 24**, the spectacle plates and lamps were mounted much lower down both 'doll' and main post for night visibility and routine maintenance.

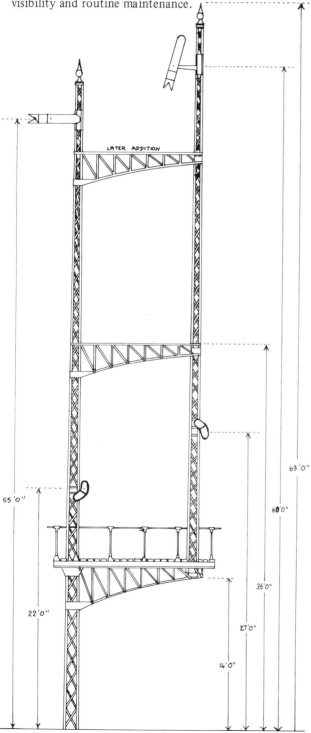

Plate 33: The crank for operating a repeating signal on a separate post from the main arm. The lever wire is at the lower right, and when pulled, both lower left and top right wires operated a home and a distant respectively.

Author

Plate 34: Repeating arms at Morningside Road, on the Edinburgh Suburban line, were connected to each other by wire, with a chain at the base around the wheel on the crank, in turn linked to the lever wire. The lower arm was less than half the length of the upper, due to restricted clearance, and, in effect, both arms compensated each other.

Author

Examples of a tall lattice post signal, without repeater and with the lamp placed level with the signal arms are depicted in the North British examples in **Plates 35 & 36**.

Mention must be made of a further method of enabling signal sighting to be readily achieved, this being the placing behind the signal arm of a fixed board, plate or slats, painted white, against which the arm moved. In some cases, no appendage was fitted, but the same objective was attained by painting a white area on the offending road bridge etc., to create the contrast. Indeed in a few instances, the yellow arm later adopted for Distant signals had a black background added to increase its visibility range, although this was the exception rather than the rule.

Where it was not possible to achieve adequate signal sighting, either by tall signals or by duplication of arms, recourse was made to repeaters mounted on separate posts. In some cases, these were ordinary arms painted white with a black band, but latterly in the pre-grouping areas, banner repeaters were used. These were similar in design to the type now in use in colour light areas, having a black band of fabric over two parallel wires and illuminated from the rear.

Plate 35: Rumbling Bridge Home signal, without repeater arm or ladder, despite its extreme height. It is also on the 'wrong' side of the track for sighting purposes.

W. S. Sellar

Plate 36: A tall North British Distant signal, on the Musselburgh branch, which was not provided with a ladder, the lamp being serviced by a 'windlass'.

J. E. Hay

White had long been recognized as an unsatisfactory colour for Clear due to the increasing possibility of confusion with other lineside lights and the inherent danger of a more restrictive spectacle glass being broken, but the main reason for its retention was the difficulty in obtaining a suitable shade of green, a problem shared with the Admiralty. In 1886, the Rules and Regulations Committee of the various railway companies recommended that green displace white and although most LNER constituents used a 'grass' green shade, when illuminated by a yellow paraffin lamp, a rather indistinct colour is said to have emerged. The Admirality developed a different shade, termed 'signal green' and this was adopted by other lines. The actual conversion to green took place in the 1890s, the Great Northern being the first major line to use red and green exclusively for main line signals, although for a short experimental period purple was tried out in lieu of green for subsidiary signals. Purple was found to be a rather poor signal colour and was discontinued.

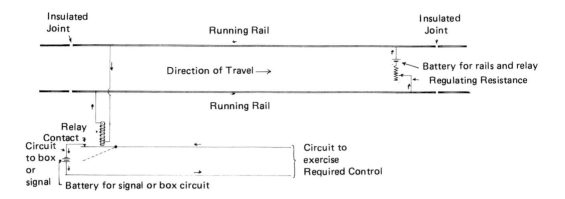

LNER TRACK CIRCUIT ELECTRICAL CIRCUIT DIAGRAM

Figure 25

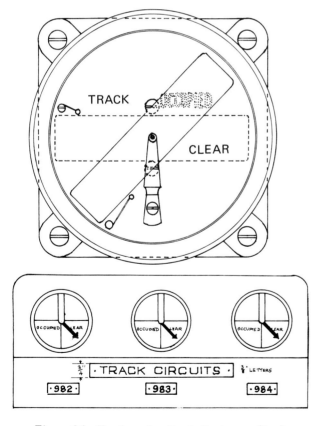

Figure 26: Track circuit indicators: (top) single and (below) mounted in a bank.

A major development in signalling practice occurred in 1894 when the Great Northern installed track circuits in the tunnels outside King's Cross. They were installed to give visual indication to a signalman of whether or not tracks under his control were clear or occupied. Early track circuit development was slow, probably due to a lack of appreciation of its potential, and also a certain degree of conservatism in using an appliance which required a degree of skill in adjusting. The full impact of their value came in 1910 after fatal accidents on the Midland Railway, which track circuits could have avoided, and thereafter expansion was rapid.

Basically, a track circuit is an electrical circuit which used the running rails as conductors. Current is essentially of small voltage, usually between 1 and 3 volts, but as this pressure could not be relied upon to bridge rail joints effectively, two bonding wires are fixed to link rail ends. If the track battery fails, or a rail breaks, the effect on the controlling circuit is the same as if the track was occupied. A simple track circuit diagram is shown in **Figure 25** and two typical signal box indicators in **Figure 26**.

In operation, current from the track battery passes through the rails with sufficient force to energize the relay circuit and coil, holding an armature in the closed position in the second circuit, thereby enabling electrical lever, etc. control to be made, and/or operating a signal box indicator.

If the line is occupied, current passes between rails via the vehicle axles, 'starving' the coil of current and losing the holding action on the second circuit, affecting different electrical controls.

Certain difficulties were experienced with Mansell-wheeled stock, which had wood segments between tyre and axle and bonding was necessary to permit current flow, as depicted in **Figure 27**.

Loss of efficiency occurs when current leaks away to 'earth', the amount being dependent on local ground conditions. Similar difficulties are experienced when light vehicles are involved, or when rails or tyres become coated with non conductive surfaces such as sand, etc., or when the bonding of Mansell wheels is defective. These factors illustrate the difficulties in maintaining a satisfactory adjustment.

Development of track circuiting made possible the safe operation of points at almost any distance from signal boxes, electrical lever locking, co-relating instruments to track conditions and facilitated the development of automatic signalling. It was also extremely valuable in indicating train positions to signalmen.

A positive step towards identification of Distant signals after dark occurred in 1898 by the introduction of the Colligny Welsh Signal Lamp, which took its name from its financier (Colligny) and patentee (Welsh). Illustrated in **Figure 28**, the lamp was used by the Great Eastern from 1906, particularly in the London area. The lamp casing incorporated a mirror which deflected some of the light from the flame to the right of the normal spectacle plate lens, providing through an opening a distinctive white ' > ' sign alongside the normal red and green lights.

Reference has been made to early experiments for signal replacement by trains, such as the Whitworth system of 1855. Several other schemes were devised, such as clockwork signals, some of which reached practical experiments, but nothing really developed.

At the end of the 19th century there was no real need in Britain for automatic signalling as most signal boxes operated connections to sidings or simple crossovers between main lines. Labour was relatively cheap, convenient and reliable. Additionally, Board of Trade Regulations had to be met and that august body would not sanction a new system until it had proved to be properly functional in a variety of operating conditions.

Line capacity in a mechanical signalling area is determined by the number of block sections, and if the latter was increased, so would be the carrying capacity. In 1901, the 11 mile stretch of double track on the North Eastern between Alne and Thirsk had six intermediate signal boxes, giving seven block sections. Bishopshouse and Sessay Wood were double line junctions, Pilmoor had a trailing connection to the Boroughbridge branch on the 'down' line, Raskelf and Sessay were stations with normal siding facilities, Codbeck existing merely to break up an otherwise long section.

Traffic volume was such that the Directors considered laying an additional running line, but their eventual decision was to install automatic signalling of the American 'Hall' pattern. The line was divided into 15 sections, each about 1,200 yards long, each section being provided with a semaphore Stop signal at its entrance with a 'slotted' Distant corresponding with the next Stop signal in advance. Point levers were 'free' if the two Stop signals in rear were at Danger, their normal position. Pulling of the point lever

locked these two signals at Danger. For the first time, an overlap was provided of 440 yards, which meant that before a Stop signal could be cleared, the section immediately ahead to the next signal and the first 440 yards of the subsequent one had to be unoccupied.

The Alne-Thirsk scheme was commissioned on 4th June, 1905, Codbeck box being removed. Raskelf and Sessay boxes then only opened to permit shunting operations. Hours of opening at Pilmoor and Bishopshouse were reduced, only Sessay Wood remaining open continuously. Cost economies, an objective of the scheme, were therefore realized.

'Hall' signals were of the electro-gas type with carbonic acid gas being used to move the arms with electricity operating the valves. Each signal consisted of six basic parts. These were the lower base for batteries; upper base for the gas mechanism; a drawn steel pillar; a collar on top of the upper base into which the pillar was stepped and cemented; the arm carrier which also formed the sockets connecting the pillar lengths and pinnacle, and the pinnacle. The base was bolted to concrete foundation.

The signals, one of which is illustrated in **Plate 37**, remained in use until 1933 when additional running lines were laid and the section resignalled with colour lights under the auspices of the LNER. Normally at Danger, the semaphores were cleared by the approach of a train if the appropriate track circuited sections ahead were not occupied. Reversion to Danger took place when a 'hold off' electrical coil was de-energized, the rest being left to gravity.

In 1909, the Great Central introduced 'Hall' electro-gas Stop and electro-motor Distant signals on the down line between Whetstone and Ashby Magna to break up an otherwise long section. A switch control was installed in Ashby Magna signal box for operation when shunting was in progress at that point, but otherwise the signals operated automatically. The electro-gas signal is shown in **Plates 38 & 39**.

A signal box in a ventilating shaft of the Great Central's Woodhead Tunnel could hardly be described as the most enticing of places for signalmen to work, and when it was closed in 1909 after a 10 year lifespan, the Company installed automatic signals in the tunnel although only applicable to freight trains, passenger workings requiring the tunnel to be clear throughout before passage.

The block section on which the signals were installed was 3 miles 416 yards long, most in the tunnel and on a rising gradient of 1 in 200. Traffic was very heavy and despite the provision of 26 tunnel ventilating shafts, the range of vision from the footplate was very restricted. Technically a double line section, 'up' and 'down' lines were in separate single line tunnels. Increasing line capacity by the laying of additional running lines was prohibitive.

The tunnel was track circuited throughout, but owing to the extremely wet conditions these were limited to lengths of 440 yards each.

The Woodhead end of the tunnel was equipped with a main signal, with a subsidiary 'warning' arm bracketed from it. When the former was cleared, it indicated that the tunnel

MANSELL WHEEL BOND

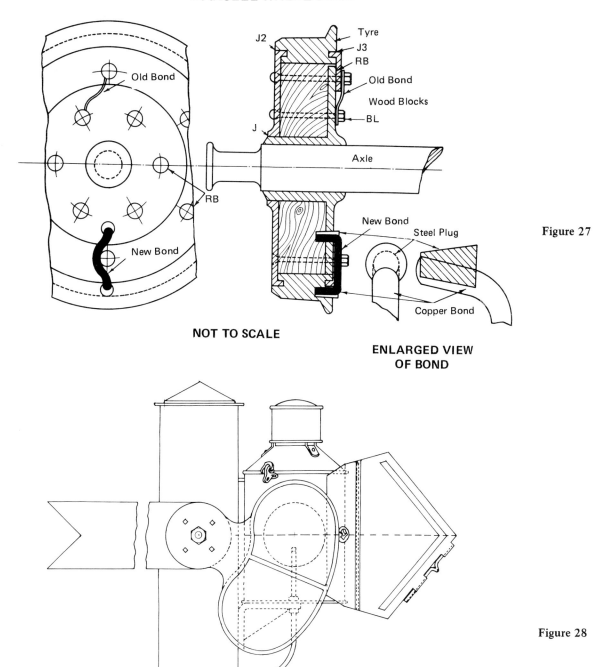

J2
Tyre
J3
RB
Old Bond
Wood Blocks
BL
J
Axle
RB
Old Bond
New Bond
Steel Plug
New Bond
Copper Bond

Figure 27

NOT TO SCALE

**ENLARGED VIEW
OF BOND**

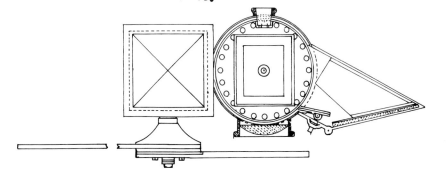

Figure 28

COLLIGNY WELSH SIGNAL LAMP

Plate 37: A Hall electro-gas signal, on the North Eastern Railway at Sessay. Note the ladder and servicing platforms are in standard North Eastern Railway style. The ground signal, in the foreground, is of McKenzie & Holland pattern.

LNER

Plates 38 and 39: A Hall electro-gas lower quadrant three position signal in the Clear position, **Plate 38** at Ashby Magna, on the Great Central Railway. **Plate 39** (inset), shows the operating mechanism in the base.

P. Tatlow Collection

was clear throughout to Dunford Bridge, but the lowering of the subsidiary arm merely indicated that the line was clear to a point some 531 yards in advance of the automatic signal in the tunnel. Both Woodhead signals were slotted by O'Donnells Rotary Slot.

An audible guide to drivers of their approach to the tunnel automatics was given by a horn some 200 yards on the approach side of each. The signals were of the electro-pneumatic type, but although normal full size spectacle plates were fitted, no arms were present, thus anticipating the LNER practice of the 1930s in mechanical colour light signals. The automatic Home signal could be controlled from the Dunford Bridge signal box and track circuit indicators for the section between Woodhead Station, and the point 531 yards past the tunnel Home, were repeated in both Woodhead East and Dunford Bridge signal boxes.

Three position upper quadrant signals appeared in 1916 on the Great Central at Keadby Bridge in Lincolnshire. In these signals, illustrated in **Plate 40**, the horizontal arm indicated Stop and had the conventional red glass, a vertical position of the arm with a green glass indicated Clear, but the 45 degree angle of the arm, indicating Caution was equipped with a yellow glass, this being claimed to be the first use of the colour in British signalling practice.

In the following years three position upper quadrant signals were installed in various isolated locations, such as Immingham (GC) in conjunction with an all electric signalling scheme, and London (King's Cross) on the GNR in 1922, as in **Plates 41 & 42**.

The introduction of upper quadrant signals did not create much confusion among drivers of the period, as apart from one or two isolated minor installations of two position upper quadrants such as at Aberdeen Station occasioned by structure gauge limitations, main line signals were almost all of the lower quadrant type.

Three position upper quadrant signals were used in lieu of mounting separate Home and Distant signals on a common post. Operating with track circuits, the vertical arm position guaranteed a clear line to the next but one Stop signal, with adequate braking distance. Unfortunately, they did not meet with universal acceptance, at least one Signal Engineer claiming that they were analogous to trying to tell the time with a single handed clock!

Plate 41: The approaches of King's Cross, in 1922, after the installation of the three aspect upper quadrant signals, by Westinghouse, two examples of which can be seen facing the camera.

Author's Collection

Plate 42: A three position upper quadrant signal at King's Cross, with route indicator and subsidiary two position upper quadrant arm. The signals were installed to improve line capacity at this Great Northern terminal in 1922.

Author's Collection

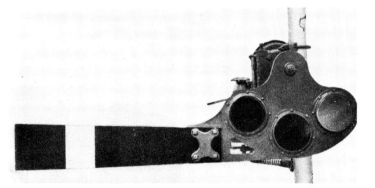

Plate 40: A British Pneumatic Signal Company three position upper quadrant arm, with the green, or right hand spectacle, plated over.

Author's Collection

The introduction of yellow to conventional Distant signal spectacle plates took place between Marylebone and Neasden, Great Central Railway, in 1916. Signal arms continued to be painted red (yellow arms came after 1925), but the hitherto white vertical stripe on the arm face was replaced by a white chevron which followed the angle of the 'V' at the end of the arm as in **Plate 43**. On the reverse side, a black chevron replaced the black stripe.

On the Great Northern, by 1922, short Home signal arms painted yellow and endorsed 'R' were used as repeaters, indicating the position of the immediately following Home signals, and working simultaneously with them.

Before considering the introduction of colour light day signals which were to quite revolutionize future signalling systems, it is as well to consider the various types of posts and fittings which characterized the purely mechanical era.

Signal posts were normally about 7 inches square at the top, tapering one-eighth of an inch outwards for each downwards foot length. A ground inset of 5 feet was considered suitable for posts up to 20 feet high, each additional 10 feet height requiring an additional 1 foot in butt length. Wood posts rested on a 6 feet crossing of 1 foot by 6 inches timber, braced diagonally between post and crossing by 9 inches by 3 inches timber. Wood post butt end preservation was by 'tarring and charring' before being fixed in position, although GNR practice was to drill the butt with a 1 inch diameter hole to a depth of 8 inches from the base, the hole being filled with fluid designed to seep outwards. Rotting butts which could not effectively be shortened were often given support below ground level with old rails. Metal posts were usually inset into the ground, and braced by 'guy' wires either set into the ground or fixed to other posts (or signals) nearby.

'Dolls' on bracket signals or gantries were usually fixed by brackets or guy wires, but on the Great Northern, they were inset into a 'pocket' in a wrought iron lattice bracket, guys being normally considered superfluous.

Plate 43: A Great Central Home and Distant signal on a concrete post. The Distant arm was painted red but with a white chevron instead of a vertical stripe, the spectacle plate glasses being yellow and green.

P. Tatlow Collection

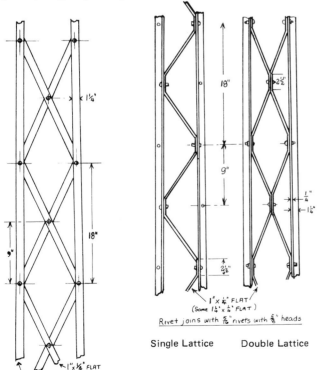

Single Lattice   Double Lattice

Figure 29: Typical lattice post construction styles and dimensions, the one on the left being particularly favoured by McKenzie & Holland.

Wood posts predominated on the Great Central, Great Eastern and Hull & Barnsley railways. The Great Northern used both wood and lattice, often in the same signal, the Great North of Scotland and North British being almost exclusively lattice, which whilst tending to have the advantage of longevity was conceded to be more difficult to alter for changing requirements. **Figure 29** depicts some lattice sizes. On the North Eastern, long wedded to wood slotted post signals (although the full slot was latterly non-functional, whenever lattice was used) it was adapted so that the arm pivoted inside the post **(See Plate 44).**

Plate 44: A small spectacled 'double lattice' signal, at Grosmont, showing the lamp mounting bracket and the pivot plate for this type of signal construction.

Author

Shortage of adequate timber supply towards the end of the First World War led to the casting at Derby for the GN and Gorton for the GC of concrete signal posts, often used in conjunction with other materials for other than simple posts. Concrete posts were comparatively expensive, difficult for erection and alteration, but durable. Great Northern signal fittings were, incidentally, made in their Peterborough foundry.

Post preservation above ground level for other than concrete posts was generally by painting. Normally the first 6 feet or so was black, the remainder being white, although the GC latterly used a stone colour. Metal parts were normally black.

Plate 45: A Great Central Railway wooden post bracket signal, at Quainton Road Junction, north of Aylesbury, where the Great Central main line to Leicester **(left)** diverged from the joint line with the Metropolitan Railway to Verney Junction. When the former opened their London extension, the junction was worked by a conventional Metropolitan Railway pattern signal box, but when this was closed, in 1921, the working of the junction was altered to be electrically operated from Quainton Road Station signal box, some 700 yards nearer to London. The 'up' junction trailing points were made spring-operated, the 'down' line (facing) points being worked by electric motors which also incorporated a detection device. The junction signals could not be cleared until the appropriate points were correctly set and a track circuit in advance, in the direction of intended travel, was not occupied. The signals were worked by electric motors which were mounted on the posts, the signal interlocking being electrical.

P. Tatlow Collection

The first use of automatic day colour light signals was on the Liverpool Overhead Railway in 1920. Great controversy arose in the signalling world over the comparative merits of the colour lights and three aspect semaphore, and A. E. Bound of the Great Central was appointed Chairman of a committee to examine and report. It was to be some time before the decision emerged in favour of colour lights.

In 1922, the Great Central prepared to deal with the increased traffic expected to arise from the 1924 Wembley Exhibition, which would traverse their Marylebone and Neasden line. A scheme was devised for resignalling with automatic day colour light signals, the locations of which were scientifically calculated, taking into account gradients, signal sighting, speed restrictions and overall running times to give a service frequency of one train each three minutes, if required. The work was jointly undertaken by GC staff and the Westinghouse Brake and Saxby Signal Coy. and using a combination of 'Hall' single lens triple aspect signals and standard multi-lens colour lights of more conventional pattern. Semaphore signalling was retained between Marylebone Station and Goods Yard signal boxes, and also beyond the Neasden South 'down' Inner Home semaphore. On the Exhibition loop, three colour light signals were provided, the outlet signal being semaphore.

In all, 13 multi-lens and 9 'searchlight' signals were installed, although in the latter case, duplicate 'repeater' signals were provided for the Marylebone Goods box 'up' Inner Homes, located inside the tunnel mouth as in **Plates 46 & 47**.

As it was considered that colour light signals could not meet the former 'splitting Distant' requirement, speed control signals were used, being basically single aspect 'searchlights' which instead of displaying a colour, showed a speed indication through a stencil. Two of this type were employed, at Neasden South for the junction to High Wycombe or Aylesbury, where '25' or '50' were respectively displayed, and at Marylebone Goods for the junction from the 'up' line to the 'up' slow/Goods Yard or along the fast line, the respective indications being '10' or '35'. The normal display was for the lower speed. These 'select speed indicators' **(Plate 48)** referred to semaphores, not colour lights, and were later replaced by banner repeaters.

The Westinghouse multi-lens signals were the first day colour light signals with more than two lenses to be installed in Great Britain for main line working. Drivers were acquainted with a yellow indication as this had been used on the section since 1916 for semaphores. All multi-lens signals **(Plates 51 & 52)** were fitted with backplates.

The 'Hall' signals were American, this being their initial British use on main lines. Illustrated in **Plates 49 & 50**, the sectional view is shown in **Figure 30**. Provision of a backplate was optional, depending on signal location as it was not thought that a dark background justified the feature. Where the signals were hung from the roof of the Lords Tunnel, only a partial backplate was provided, the co-acting ground level repeaters being unequipped. Different colours were displayed by a vane with three colour glasses,

red being the central colour and also being in the position to which the vane would revert by gravity in the event of relay failure. The lens was ten and a half inches in diameter, the vane glasses being one inch in diameter and one sixteenth of an inch thick. A 6 volt double filament bulb was used with a special 'cut in' relay to illuminate the second filament on the failure of the first.

Automatic signals were numbered by the distance in yards from the buffer stops at Marylebone Station, using only the first two digits, and suffixed 'A'. Semi-automatic signals had the letter 'A' illuminated from the rear when automatic conditions applied, as in **Plate 49**.

Prior to commissioning the colour lights, the GC had installed "Reliostop" train control gear at semaphore signals on the line and this was retained in full for the Neasden mechanical signals. The feature of a full 'stop' was not considered necessary for the automatic signals, but a 'fixed Distant' lineside apparatus was installed to give automatic brake application and sound the horn in the cab when a locomotive was 10 seconds running time in rear of a signal, even if a green aspect was displayed. A 'cancelling' facility enabled the driver to over-ride the brake application.

The full colour light scheme was commissioned in 1923, the final cost being £15,955, an overspending of £2,655, generally attributable to the excess spending of £2,719 by the railway staff element.

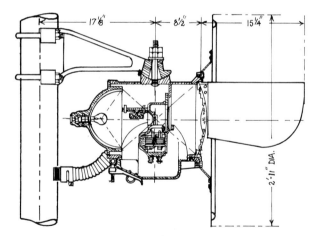

Figure 30: A sectional elevation of a Hall three aspect 'searchlight' signal, as used in the Marylebone and Neasden 1922 Great Central resignalling scheme.

Plate 48: 'Select Speed Indicator' signals which referred to semaphores. They were formed by adaptation of the searchlight signal principle.

Plate 50: A Hall searchlight single lens multi-aspect signal with backplate, as used on the Wembley Exhibition loop line.

Plate 51: A 'conventional' multilens Westinghouse day colour light signal, used on the Marylebone to Neasden resignalling scheme.

Plate 52: The 4.30 p.m. ex-Marylebone, passes the signal shown in **Plate 51** (above).

Plate 49 (left): A three aspect Hall searchlight signal, without backplate, with a small illuminated 'A' sign mounted below, indicating that the signal was operating automatically. If the sign was not lit, the signal would be fully controlled by a signal box.

Plate 46 (above left): A rear view of Hall searchlight signals, at Marylebone, from the 1922 Great Central Railway resignalling scheme. The main signals (roof suspended) have ground level repeaters to guard against smoke obscuring the former.

P. Tatlow Collection

Plate 47 (below left): A view from inside the tunnel mouth showing the signals in **Plate 46**, looking towards Marylebone.

P. Tatlow Collection

Plate 53: The main lower quadrant signal is of Great Central origin, but the bracket, of GC pattern, is a post-grouping addition. The arm on the bracket doll is of Great Eastern type while the signal box has its origin in the Metropolitan Railway (later absorbed by the LNER in 1936). The location is Quainton Road, on the Met. & GC Joint line, north of Aylesbury.

N. D. Mundy

Plate 54: Platform starting signals, of the Great Central type, at the platform ends of the London Marylebone terminus. The full post mounting arrangement of the left hand subsidiary is of interest, as is the placing of the track circuit 'diamonds' above the main signal arms.

N. D. Mundy

Plate 55: The Great Central signal gantry, at Marylebone, with station signal box in the background. These were the first signals after leaving the terminus, the 'ringed' arms controlling entry to the 'down' slow line, the others the 'down' fast. The arms, whose reverse side is toward the camera, control entry to the platforms from the left, 'up' slow, and right, 'up' main. Platform 2 was accessible from either.

Author's Collection

Plate 57: A close up of the spectacle plate arm spindle lamp holder and 'back blinder' of the signal shown in **Plate 56**.

Author

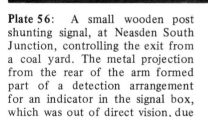

Plate 56: A small wooden post shunting signal, at Neasden South Junction, controlling the exit from a coal yard. The metal projection from the rear of the arm formed part of a detection arrangement for an indicator in the signal box, which was out of direct vision, due to the presence of a road overbridge.

Author

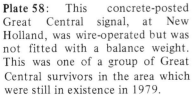

Plate 58: This concrete-posted Great Central signal, at New Holland, was wire-operated but was not fitted with a balance weight. This was one of a group of Great Central survivors in the area which were still in existence in 1979.

Author

Plate 59: Common post-mounted shunting signals, at New Holland, with balance weights immediately below the arms. The arms were for diverging lines, the top arm referring to the line furthest to the left. The numbers on the post refer to operating lever numbers.

Author

Plate 60: A rear view of the signals in **Plate 59** showing the cut-out on the curved 'back light blinders'. Note the shape of the balance weights.

Author

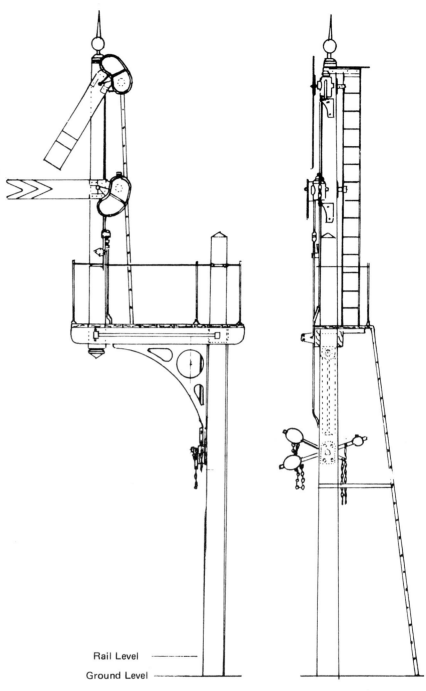

Figure 31: A sketch of a Great Central bracket signal fitted with Home and Distant signal arms.

Plate 61: A Great Central lower quadrant signal in Lincolnshire. Note the use of the 'open ball' finial on the wood post, similar to the Stevens pattern found on the northern lines of the LNER constituents.

G. Toole

Plate 62: Signals at Dereham South Junction on the Great Eastern Railway. They are on separate posts with an extended bracket for staging, for convenience of access to left hand post arms.

J. Watling

Plate 63: Two subsidiary arms 'Shunt' and 'Loop', on independent posts, in this bracket signal at Dereham North. Note the balance weight arrangement.

J. Watling

Plate 65: The 'Main', 'Calling on' and 'Goods Loop' signals on a bracket signal at Yarmouth South Town, with a single post, double armed signal behind. All signals are of Great Eastern pattern.

J. Watling

Plate 64: Great Eastern Railway type platform starting signals at Yarmouth South Town. Note the balance weight arrangement to allow for clearances.

J. Watling

Plate 66: Newmarket Old was shunted by a horse, accompanied by a shunter on foot, and this explains the reason for the low height of the arm (for sighting purposes). The restricted space in which the signal operated was responsible for the short arm and also the unusual 'off centre' location of the balance weight.

J. Watling

Plate 67: One main and two subsidiary arms on a common post at Beccles. The centre arm was provided to permit access to the water tower in the background without lowering the main (top) arm. The lower signal was of the 'shunt ahead' subsidiary, allowing a train to pass the main arm at 'Danger' for the purpose of setting back into the line to the left.

J. Watling

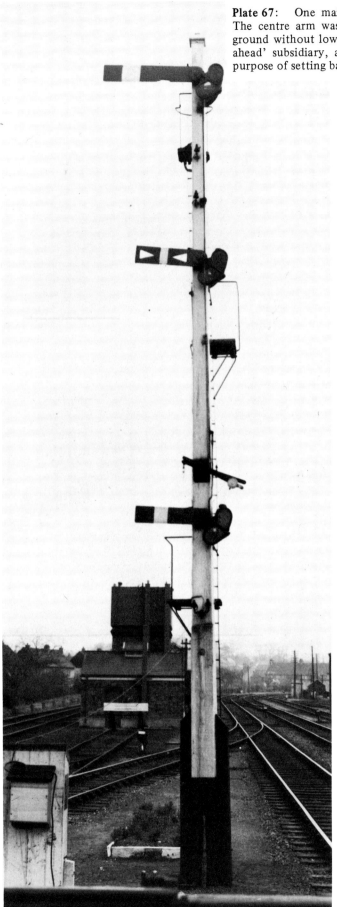

Plate 68: A wood post with an iron bracket bracing on these Great Eastern type signals at Beccles. The shunting signal is of L N E R type.

J. Watling

Plate 69: A common base five arm Great Eastern type signal at Millwall Junction, where the routes from Fenchurch Street to North Greenwich and Blackwall diverged. The Midland Railway used the latter line to gain access to Poplar Docks.

J. Watling

Plate 70: An Annet type mechanical route indicator, with a five route display potential, mounted under a standard Great Eastern 'Home' arm at Millwall Junction, London. This obviated complicated bracket or gantry construction when space was restricted. Routes were shown either as letters or numbers, (or both).

J. Watling

Plate 72 (right): This Great Eastern Railway subsidiary ▷ signal had the letters 'STOP SHUNT' screwed to the approach side to protect the loop and goods shed entrance (far left background) from coal yard shunting in the sidings behind the photographer. St. Botolph's Yard, Colchester is the location.

J. Watling

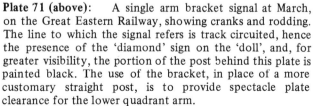

Plate 71 (above): A single arm bracket signal at March, on the Great Eastern Railway, showing cranks and rodding. The line to which the signal refers is track circuited, hence the presence of the 'diamond' sign on the 'doll', and, for greater visibility, the portion of the post behind this plate is painted black. The use of the bracket, in place of a more customary straight post, is to provide spectacle plate clearance for the lower quadrant arm.

J. Watling

Plate 73 (right): Common post-mounted Great Eastern ▷ 'Distants', at Wells Gate, the upper arm being 'fixed' at Caution. Note that the upper arm is longer than the one below and is not fitted with a spectacle plate.

J. Watling

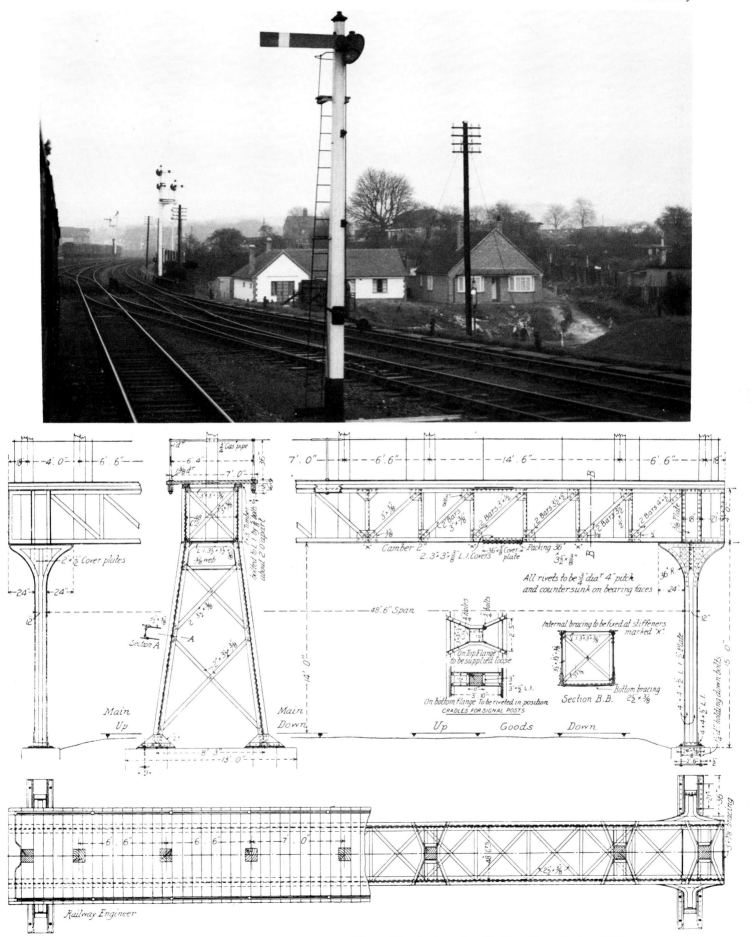

Plate 74: A 'down' starting signal, on the Great Eastern Railway, at Newmarket. All other signals are also of GE pattern.

P. J. Kelley

Figure 32: An iron signal bridge, Great Eastern Railway.

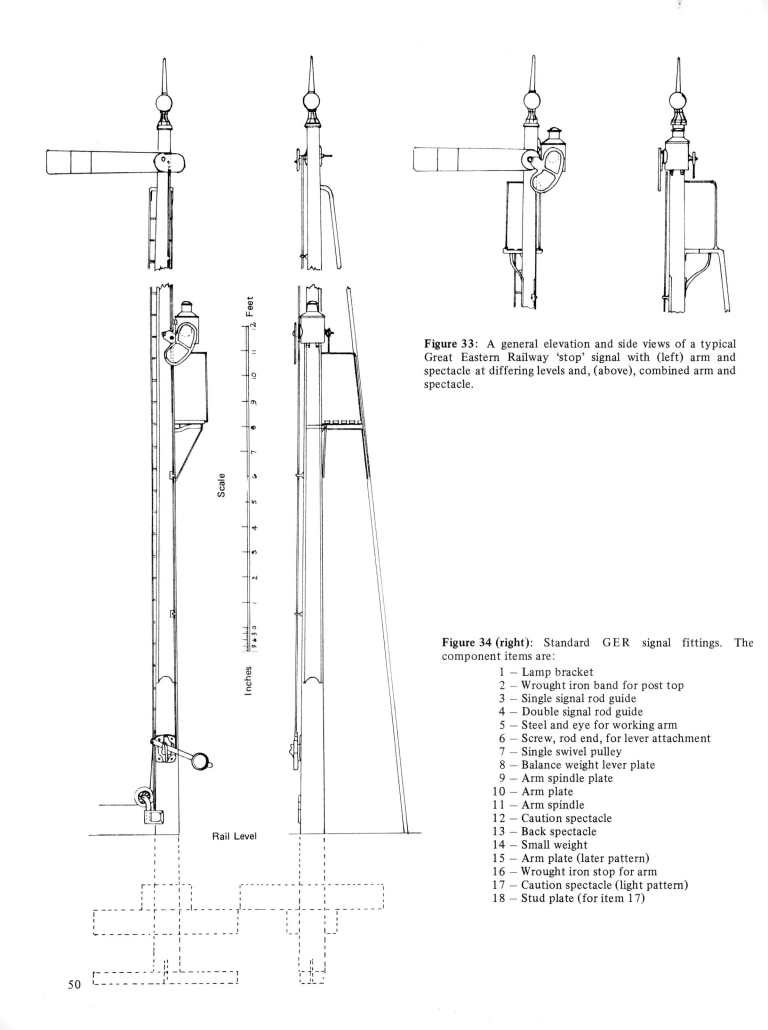

Figure 33: A general elevation and side views of a typical Great Eastern Railway 'stop' signal with (left) arm and spectacle at differing levels and, (above), combined arm and spectacle.

Figure 34 (right): Standard GER signal fittings. The component items are:

1 – Lamp bracket
2 – Wrought iron band for post top
3 – Single signal rod guide
4 – Double signal rod guide
5 – Steel and eye for working arm
6 – Screw, rod end, for lever attachment
7 – Single swivel pulley
8 – Balance weight lever plate
9 – Arm spindle plate
10 – Arm plate
11 – Arm spindle
12 – Caution spectacle
13 – Back spectacle
14 – Small weight
15 – Arm plate (later pattern)
16 – Wrought iron stop for arm
17 – Caution spectacle (light pattern)
18 – Stud plate (for item 17)

Scale

Feet

Inches

Rail Level

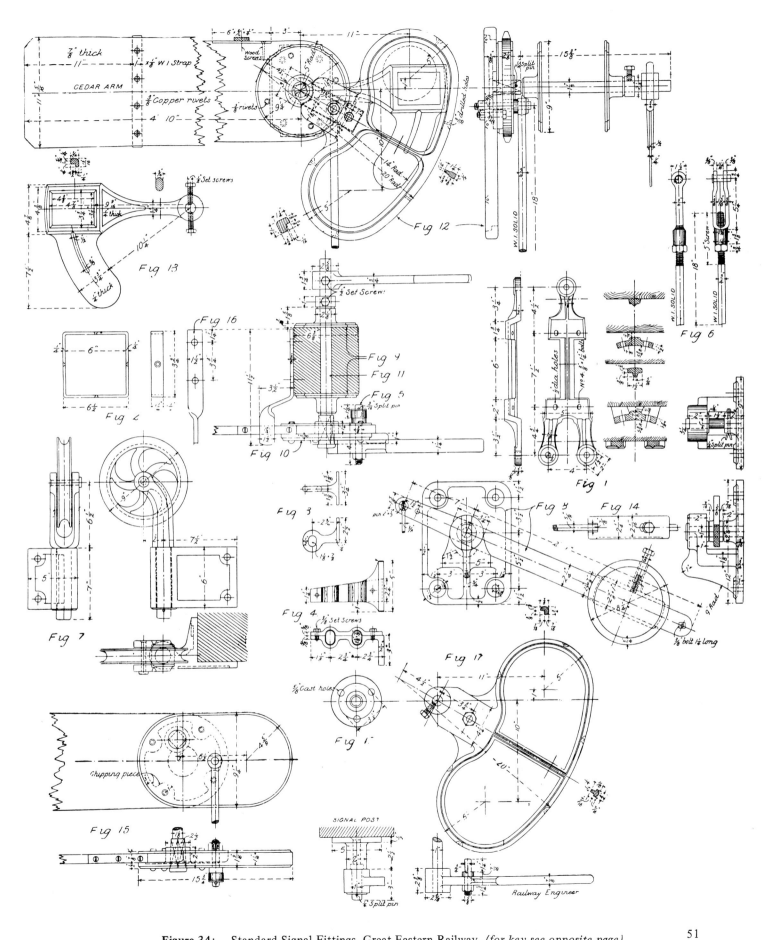

Figure 34: Standard Signal Fittings, Great Eastern Railway. *(for key see opposite page)*

51

Plate 75: A single arm lattice post 'somersault' signal, for trains approaching from Sleaford, at Hubberts Bridge on the Great Northern Railway. Note the Great Northern fencing.

J. Evans

Plate 76: A lattice post double arm 'somersault', on the Great Northern Railway, at Rauceby.

J. Evans

Plate 77: Two Great Northern Railway 'somersaults' both with the arm and lamp on different levels and both mounted on concrete posts. The location is Honnington Junction, between Barkston and Sleaford.

Crown Copyright, National Railway Museum

Plate 78: An all lattice bracket signal, with later type of corrugated steel arm, at Willoughby on the Great Northern Railway.

J. Evans

Plate 80: A lattice junction signal, with the left hand arm almost at the theoretical vertical position for Clear, at Potters Bar in 1929.

Photomatic

Plate 79: A rear view of the signal arm, showing fittings, as seen in **Plate 78**.

J. Evans

Plate 81: Two vertically-mounted main line 'somersaults' on a wooden post, providing for two routes without resort to a bracket arrangement, at Firsby, on the Great Northern Railway.

J. Evans

Plate 82: A concrete post-mounted 'somersault' at Cuffley Station on the Great Northern Railway.

P. J. Kelley

Plate 83 (above right): A concrete construction post bracket signal at Burgh-le-Marsh, Great Northern Railway.

J. Evans

Plate 84: Concrete post-mounted 'somersault' signal arms, at Spalding, Great Northern Railway. The subsidiary arm was top-mounted for routing, not precedence. Note the holes below the main arm for a removed second arm.

Author's Collection

Plates 85 and 86: Front and rear views of a standard Great North of Scotland signal at Alford. The signal lamp has been lowered on the windlass.

W. S. Sellar

Plate 87: A McKenzie & Holland lower quadrant at Aberdeen Joint Station. Space restraints required the signal to be roof-suspended with base finial.

Author

Plate 88: A Great North of Scotland Railway bracket signal with telegraph post 'doll'.

J. Emslie Collection

Plate 89: A Great North of Scotland Railway double-armed subsidiary signal at Kittybrewster South.

Author

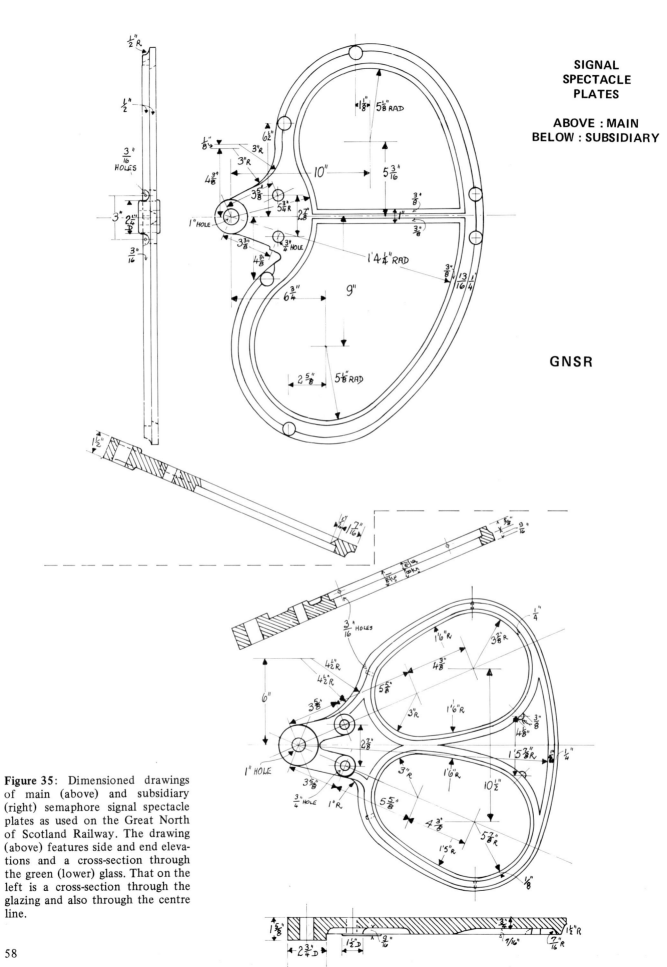

SIGNAL
SPECTACLE
PLATES

ABOVE : MAIN
BELOW : SUBSIDIARY

GNSR

Figure 35: Dimensioned drawings of main (above) and subsidiary (right) semaphore signal spectacle plates as used on the Great North of Scotland Railway. The drawing (above) features side and end elevations and a cross-section through the green (lower) glass. That on the left is a cross-section through the glazing and also through the centre line.

Plate 90: A short Home and Distant and a normal Home, with signal numbers attached to the front of the left hand post, at Sandholme, on the Hull & Barnsley Railway.

C. T. Goode

Plate 91: A wood bracket signal, with the right hand 'doll' removed, at Kirk Smeaton, on the Hull & Barnsley main line.
C. T. Goode

Plate 92: A wood post Hull & Barnsley Railway fixed Distant, at Sprotborough.

C. T. Goode

Plate 93: A Hull & Barnsley Railway wood post signal, prior to its replacement by the tubular post alongside, at Springhead, Hull.

M. R. Lake

Plate 94: A wood gantry near Springbank, Hull. Angle cranks are not used in the wire run to the centre 'doll'. Note the balance weight positioning for clearances and the minimum horizontal arm clearance.

Plate 95:   A suspended Home signal, at Trinity Junction, Edinburgh. The signal was outside a tunnel mouth and the unusual construction was dictated by sighting requirements.

Author

Plate 96:   A bridge-mounted lower quadrant, with sighting board, on the Forth Bridge.

Photomatic

Plate 97:   Glenburnie Junction, North Fife, with a conventional North British Home signal and tablet platforms with oil location lamps.

W. A. C. Smith

Plate 98: Home and Distant North British Railway arms on a common post at Shore Road, Stirling. Both arms are at Clear.

W. S. Sellar

Plate 99: Corpach North British Railway Distant signal. No ladder is fitted, but the windlass chain can be clearly seen passing through the lattice post. Note the white painting of the spectacle plate.

P. J. Kelley

Plate 100: Winkston Level Crossing, on the Peebles line, North British Railway, with two standard Home signals for protection. Both signals and their Distants were worked from the crossing keeper's house on the right.

W. A. C. Smith

Plate 102: A Stevens lattice post junction signal, with North British arm on the left and a McKenzie & Holland arm on the right, at Lumphinnans Central Junction, Fife.

W. A. C. Smith

Plate 101 (above left): A North British 'Calling on' arm at St. Margarets Locomotive Depot outlet, Edinburgh. The ladder is used as a bracing strut, and the lamp is non-standard.

Author

Plate 103: An 'open scissors' type arm for 'back shunt' purposes at Prestonpans, on the North British. The ladder is not of NBR pattern and was a later addition to enable the windlass to be discontinued.

J. E. Hay

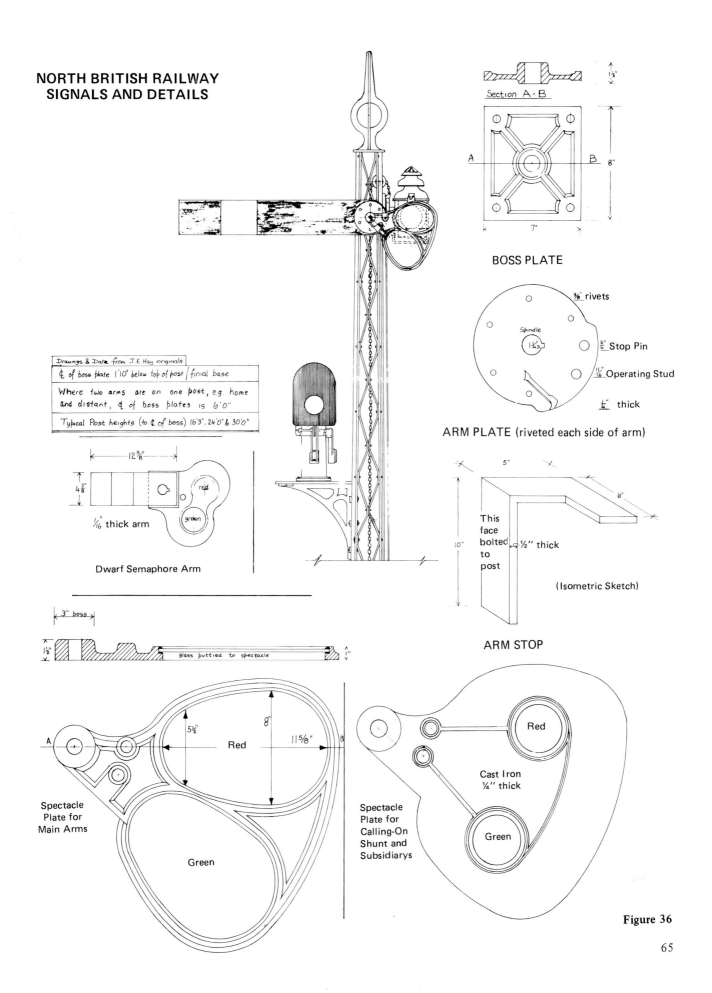

NORTH BRITISH RAILWAY
SIGNALS AND DETAILS

Section A - B

$1\frac{1}{2}''$

BOSS PLATE

8"

7"

$\frac{3}{8}''$ rivets

Spindle

$1\frac{1}{2}''$

$\frac{3}{4}''$ Stop Pin

$\frac{11}{16}''$ Operating Stud

$\frac{1}{4}''$ thick

ARM PLATE (riveted each side of arm)

Drawings & Data from J E Hay originals

₵ of boss plate 1'10" below top of post / finial base

Where two arms are on one post, e.g. home and distant, ₵ of boss plates is 6'0"

Typical Post heights (to ₵ of boss) 16'3", 24'0" & 30'0"

5"

6"

This face bolted to post

$\frac{1}{2}''$ thick

10'

(Isometric Sketch)

$12\frac{3}{8}''$

$4\frac{3}{8}''$

red

green

$\frac{1}{16}''$ thick arm

Dwarf Semaphore Arm

ARM STOP

3" boss

$1\frac{1}{2}''$

1"

glass puttied to spectacle

A

$5\frac{1}{2}''$

8"

$11\frac{5}{8}''$

Red

B

Green

Spectacle Plate for Main Arms

Red

Cast Iron $\frac{1}{4}''$ thick

Green

Spectacle Plate for Calling-On Shunt and Subsidiarys

Figure 36

Plate 105 (above): A slotted post signal, with round spectacle plates and a plate to prevent false indications, near Newcastle. Surmounted by an unusual finial, the arm was red with a black band.

Author

Plate 104 (above left): A North Eastern Railway wood bracket signal and water column. Additional bracing for the main post of the signal is provided from the smaller post in front.

Author

Plate 106: A restored wood post signal of the North Eastern Railway type on the North York Moors Railway at Goathland. Note the modern 'theatre' type route indicator installed after 'privatisation.'

Author

Plate 107: A lower quadrant signal of NE pattern, fitted with a steel arm of modern pattern functioning as a fixed Distant, on the Esk Valley line. Both spectacle glasses have been broken, and the finial has been removed.

Author

Plate 108: This restored wooden bracket signal, of North Eastern Railway type, at Goathland, displaced a modern welded steel structure when the North York Moors Railway passed to the preservation trust.

Author

Plate 109: A fine main line North Eastern Railway signal, at Coldstream, with the balance weight in the elevated position. Note the 'ball and spike' finial.

J. E. Hay

Plate 110: A small arm 'slotted post' signal, at Leyburn, on the North Eastern Railway, with large spectacle glasses, mounted on a lattice post. The wooden finial was hacked, rather crudely, from a solid block of wood.

G. Toole

Plate 111: Apart from two upper quadrant arms on the gantry to the left, the signalling at York, in this 1937 view, is pure North Eastern.

LNER

Plate 112: Redundant main line arms were removed from this North Eastern Railway signal, at Tynemouth, leaving spectacle plates only. The small arms were for 'facing road' moves.

Author

Plate 113: The base of a North Eastern Railway signal, at Coldstream, showing the use of angle cranks and rigid coupling to the balance weight arm, in lieu of the more usual wire (or chain) and wheel. The signal box lever number is displayed on the post.

J. E. Hay

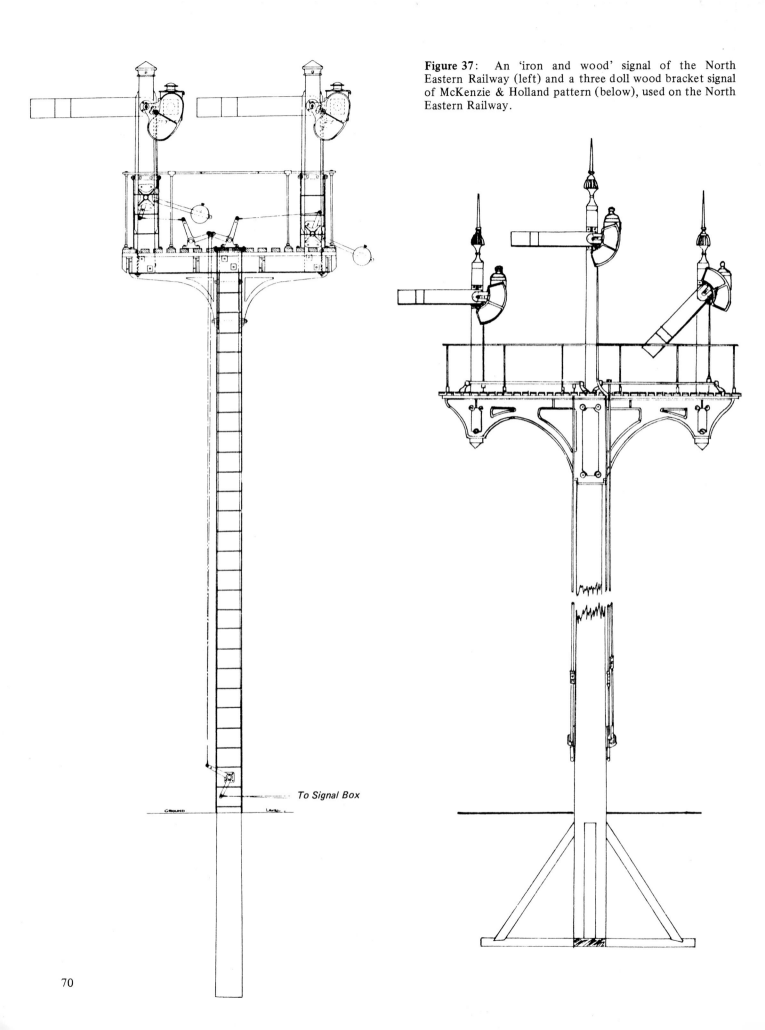

Figure 37: An 'iron and wood' signal of the North Eastern Railway (left) and a three doll wood bracket signal of McKenzie & Holland pattern (below), used on the North Eastern Railway.

To Signal Box

GROUND   LEVEL

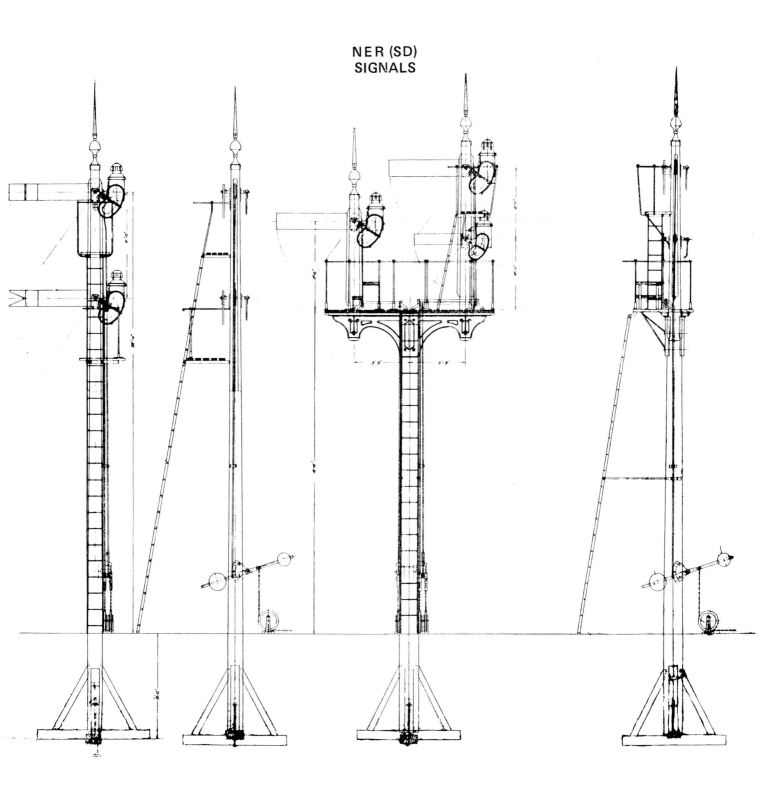

Figure 38: Drawings of Southern Division signals of the North Eastern Area, showing the total wooden post height, including the portion below ground level, which rested on a cruciform wood base and was braced diagonally. In both side elevations, lampholders and lamps have been omitted. The finial, surmounting both signals, is of the McKenzie & Holland large type, although spectacle plates and signal arms are of NER pattern. Note the inclusion of platforms for lamp servicing for all arms, including the upper arm on the right hand doll of the bracket signal.

Chapter Two

Ground Signals

Ground Signals

Ground signals evolved initially to give route setting information, one of the first being the Stevens example in **Plate 114**. The red blade of the signal was directly linked to the point blades and moved in unison. Initially without lamps, one was later inset into the post and a red/green/red spectacle plate fitted as in **Figure 39**. Correctly set points gave a green indication, but if not fully over, a small portion of red glass was illuminated.

Saxby developed this device into a form of semaphore signal with two lamps but one red/green/red spectacle plate as in **Figure 40**. Point setting controlled the arm as before, but after dark, travel direction was indicated by a combination of two lights. The red glass was much wider than the green and both arms were endorsed with the route to which they referred. The 'droop' of the 'permitting' arm was identical to the Caution aspect of the contemporary three position semaphore.

The height of the Saxby indicator signal was liable to cause confusion with main line signals, so smaller types evolved only a few feet high. Point blade operated, a disadvantage was that when two were provided, as at crossovers, conflicting signals could be given. Saxby therefore produced a device to enable signalmen to pre-select the signal to be cleared by a lever mounted on the point lever in the frame. Lever space was also saved as one point and two signal levers were combined into the space of a single lever. The device is shown in **Figure 41**.

Saxby signal miniaturization produced the 'Duplex Ground Disc Signal' **(Figure 42)** still using two lamps. Meanwhile, single lamp indicators were developing using discs, or 'targets' in place of arms. In some examples, e.g. **Plate 115**, the disc was fitted to the lamp housing, the entire unit rotating. In others, only the disc rotated as in **Plate 116**. The discs were painted the same colour as the lens, or coloured glass inset where the lamp was stationary. Spectacle plate size was reduced to avoid any confusion with main line signals, particularly when sighting required signal elevation. A rotating lamp disadvantage was that movement vibration could extinguish the flame.

Ground signals became independent of points and, although separate levers were required, siting was simplified. Signals were fitted with balance weights to restore them to their most restrictive aspect and detection equipment prevented clearance unless point settings were complete.

An alternative to discs was provided in some cases by miniature semaphores, as in **Plates 117 & 118**, certain GCR examples being fitted with rubber arms for staff safety. **Figure 43** is a double arm variation of the signal in **Plate 118**, and is drawn as mounted on a 'T' section post.

On the Great Central and Great Eastern discs, the targets were attached to the lamp, examples of the latter are in **Plates 119–121**. Great Northern ground signals were of the type in **Figure 44 & Plate 122**, the lamp unit and discs moving through a right angle. In latter years, some of this type of ground signal had the disc overpainted to show a red band on white, horizontally for Stop and at an

upward angle for Clear, in the latter case with a disc being specially provided with one chord removed as in **Plate 123**. A semaphore Hull & Barnsley ground signal is shown in **Plate 124**. Most Scottish ground signals were of Stevens' pattern, the major differences being in the shape of the faceplate which hinged downwards externally, and the provision of green spectacle glasses inside the main casting on the GNSR, but externally in the NB. The GNS type is shown in **Figure 45** the NB in **Figure 46** and **Plates 125 & 126**. A typical North Eastern Railway ground signal was the product of McKenzie & Holland type and is shown in **Figure 47 & Plate 127**. Different lamp casings could be found on the NE according to the signalling division concerned.

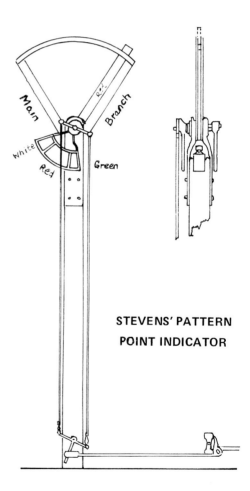

STEVENS' PATTERN
POINT INDICATOR

Figure 39: Although not strictly a true signal, the function of this piece of equipment was to indicate to a driver the position of point blades, to which it was directly coupled. Not all 'signals' of this type were equipped with lamps and red/green glasses, this being a later addition. An illustration of this signal can be found in **Plate 114**.

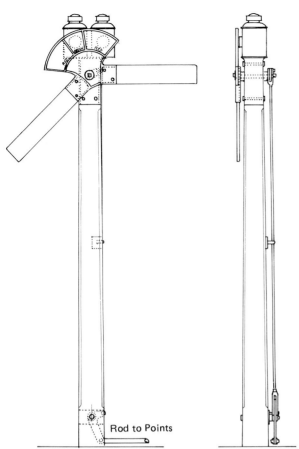

R = Red Glass
G = Green Glass

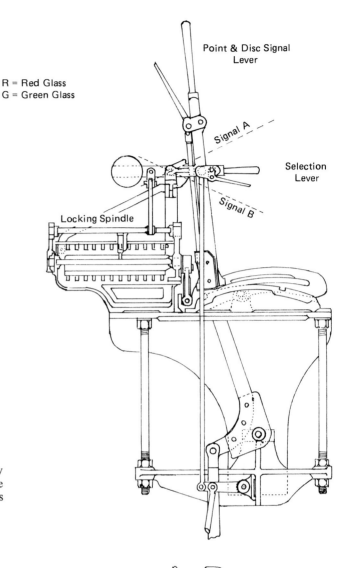

Point & Disc Signal
Lever

Signal A

Selection
Lever

Signal B

Locking Spindle

Figure 40: The Saxby point indicator was directly coupled, by rodding, to the point blades, and when the latter were correctly set, a red and green indication was given, the green being to the same side as the lowered arm.

Rod to Points

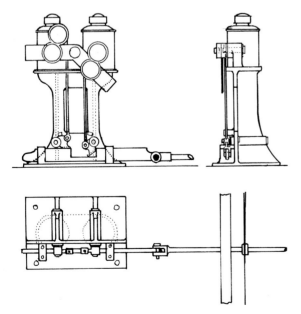

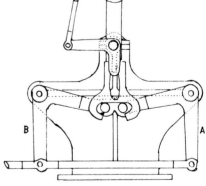

B   A

Figure 41: A Saxby pattern, in which the main point lever had an additional horizontal lever fitted adjacent to it, which enabled selection of the ground signal according to direction of travel. All were fully interlocked with each other.

Figure 42: The Duplex ground disc was a development of that in **Figure 40**, where each arm carried its own coloured spectacle plates.

Plate 115: A rotating head ground signal with the red 'target' fixed to the lamp and the adjacent side painted white. When 'cleared', the lamp rotated ninety degrees on its base. This signal is preserved, at Grosmont, by the North York Moors Railway.

Author

Plate 114 (above left): An early Stevens direction indicator signal, without lamp or spectacle plate, preserved in the North Road Station Museum, Darlington.

Author

Plate 116: A fixed lamp, but rotating targets feature in this ground signal, now in the National Railway Museum at York.

Author

Plate 117: A Great Central electro-pneumatic ground signal working in the lower quadrant. Rubber arms were fitted to safeguard staff.

P. Tatlow Collection

Plate 118: A Railway Signal Company ground shunting signal, with the yellow arm and black stripe for moves into the 'headshunt', with the arm at Danger, at Roxburgh Junction.

J. E. Hay

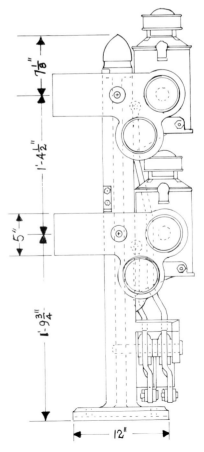

Figure 43: A Railway Signal Company two arm ground signal, mounted on the front of a 'T' section solid post.

Plate 122: A Great Northern Railway ground signal, with controlling lever number cast into the face, for a movement over trailing points. To the rear, is a standard LNER ground disc signal.

A. Waterfall

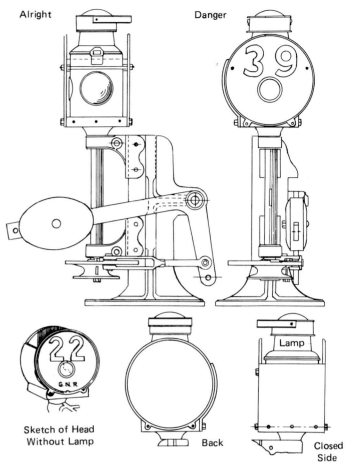

Alright   Danger

Sketch of Head Without Lamp   Back   Lamp   Closed Side

GREAT NORTHERN RAILWAY STANDARD GROUND DISC SIGNAL.

Figure 44 (above): Side 'Alright and end 'Danger' elevation of a standard GNR ground disc signal, supplemented by an iso metric sketch of the head unit without the lamp, and views of the rear and closed side, complete. Note that no provision is made for a 'backlight' arrangement. The numbers shown on the drawings of working faces (39 & 22) were embossed into the disc and indicate the lever number in the signal box frame which controlled the operation of the signal. In practice, the length of the rod, which linked the lamp with the balance weight was variable according to signal sighting requirements, and examples are known where this rod exceeded 6 ft.

Plate 123: Originally a Great Northern Railway ground disc signal, of the type illustrated above, this example has had the original lamp unit replaced by a standard LNER lamp, with an additional lens in the side at right angles to the normal. Metal round plates were bolted to the lamp, the full face being white with a horizontal red bar, and indicating 'stop'. The other (adjacent) disc had a chord cut away, as in the illustration, the red bar being inclined as upper quadrant indicating 'Clear'. The lens in the former side was red and that in the latter, green. The entire lamp and discs unit rotated as in the original.

Auth

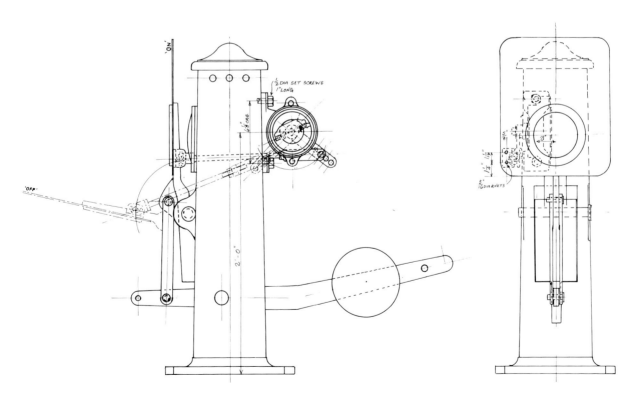

Figure 45: A Great North of Scotland ground signal of Stevens' pattern with the spectacle plate within the main lamp casing. When 'cleared', the front flap, which contained a clear lens, fell forward. The device on the rear of the casing is a signal detector which gave an indication, in the controlling signal box, of the signal position, and was optional according to signal location.

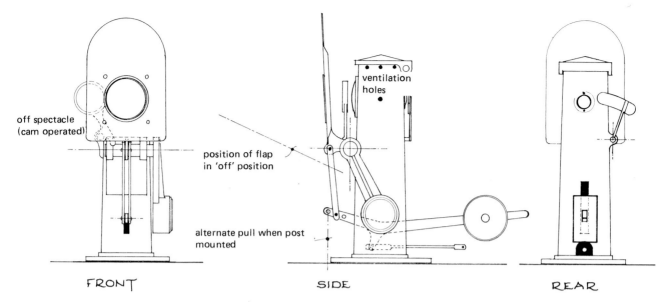

off spectacle
(cam operated)

position of flap
in 'off' position

alternate pull when post
mounted

ventilation
holes

FRONT   SIDE   REAR

Operation : when flap drops, "off" spectacle drops to fall
over spectacle to show white light (N.B.R days) green (LNER days)
operated by simple cam.
Colour Flap Red otherwise white all over.

NORTH BRITISH RLY
Standard Shunt Signal (Stevens' type)

Figure 46

Plate 125: A standard Stevens ground signal, of the North British Railway, in the Clear position with the green spectacle plate glass in position over the Clear lens. The red 'target' was lowered.

R. Montgomery

Plate 126: A rear view of a sleeper-mounted Stevens signal, showing the backlight 'blinder' and balance weight shot.

Author

Plate 127: A standard McKenzie & Holland ground signal, on the Northern Division of the North Eastern Railway, with rotating head.

J. E. Hay

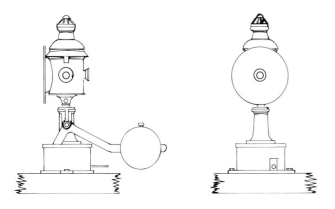

**McKENZIE & HOLLAND TYPE
GROUND DISC SIGNAL**

Figure 47: A side elevation and end view of a standard McKenzie & Holland ground disc signal, as used on the North Eastern Railway. Lamp patterns varied according to the signalling area in which they were used.

Chapter Three

Detection, Point Locking and Signal Slotting

Detection

The function of detection apparatus is to ensure that facing points are correctly set for movements to or from running lines before the protecting signal can be cleared.

Probably the first example of its kind was installed at East Retford in 1852, although this was only applicable to one signal at one set of points for one of two alternative directions. It was extremely elementary, but the principle was established which was to be developed over the ensuing years. The East Retford installation comprised a flat bar of metal which was affixed to the point blade, passing through the stock rail to an adjacent signal which was operated by a down rod. This rod was extended so that it passed through a hole in the bar when the signal could be cleared. If the points were reversed, the hole was not in alignment with the down rod and signal clearance could not be given. As a corollary, when the signal down rod engaged in the hole in the point bar, the points could not be moved. The arrangement is depicted in **Figure 48**.

The vertical movement of the signal down rod was later altered to a horizontal movement in the run of signal wires depicted in **Figures 49 & 50**, ('goose neck' and 'notch' locks) and also in **Plates 128–131**, according to complexity.

With the development of the plunger bolt at facing points, it became a Ministry of Transport requirement that this apparatus was also detected in a similar manner to the actual point blades before the appropriate signal could be cleared **(Plate 132)**.

The development of electrically-operated points and signals led to electrical detection apparatus, which did not require the same degree of attention in fine setting that was called for by mechanical means. On the other hand, electrical detection did not physically hold the points in position when signals had been cleared as in mechanical systems, but locked the lever electrically.

Plate 128: A simple 'notch' locking, incorporated in the run of the signal wire, running from bottom to top. The horizontal bar is attached to the point tie bar.

Author

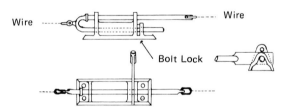

Figure 49: 'Goose Neck' slotting by metallic strip in a signal wire 'run' engaged with a bar extending from the point blades.

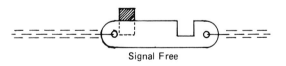

Signal Free

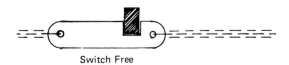

Switch Free

Figure 50: 'Notch' slotting, operated in a similar manner to 'Goose Neck', but this was simpler in installation. This is illustrated in **Plate 128 (above)**.

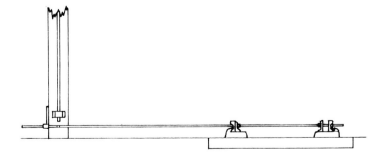

Figure 48: The arrangement at East Retford, in 1852, where a metal bar linked to the point blades extended to an adjacent signal. The bar had two holes drilled to allow the signal operating rod extension to penetrate for full arm movement when the points were correctly set.

Plate 129: An expansion of the 'notch lock', involving the locking of a ground signal with two sets of points. As in **Plate 128**, the wire to lock attachments are of a simple type.

Author

Plate 130: Clearance of the signal, in this case, is dependent upon three separate points, one at either end of a crossover and a set of catch points, being in correct alignment. Note the adjusting device comprising a threaded rod passing through a plate bolted above the signal wire bar, for the signal wire, fitted to the unit at the right hand end, the left being a simple coupling.

Author

Plate 131: A more complicated form of 'notch lock' arrangement, incorporating signal balance weights in advance of the locking, but ground-mounted. This example was at Doncaster. Ground mounting of signal balance weights was resorted to in areas of restricted clearance or when the more customary post mounting could not be provided due to the number of arms requiring complicated slotting.

Author

Plate 132: The interior of a combined facing point lock and point detector, of LNER vintage, but incorporating electrical contacts.

LNER

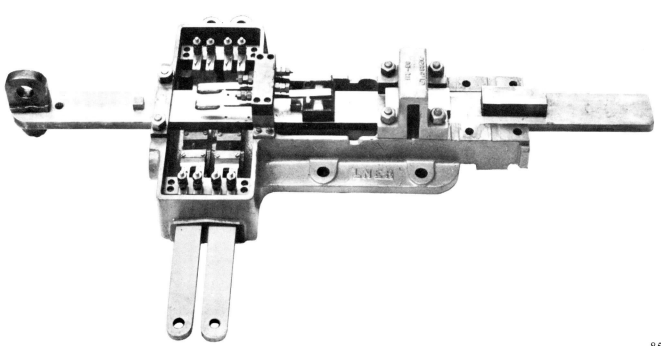

Locking of Points

Interlocking development promoted a sense of security with signalmen, but could do nothing to prevent points moving under a passing train, or even the actions of forgetful signalmen moving points whilst a trains was traversing them. Indeed, facing point provision was considered as an activity to be avoided at all costs, in the first four decades of railways. In 1874, the NE main line from York to Berwick (160 miles) had only three facing points, other than at main stations.

The first facing point locking apparatus was devised by Joseph Hill, a fitter with Stevens, about 1866. Essentially it was a series of long armed cranks, all coupled to the points by one rod. When points moved, the long ends were raised above rail level, but depressable by train passage when the points were unable to be moved. Hill presented his ideas to the firm, but no interest was apparently shown.

In 1867, William Stroudley patented a device for preventing locomotive wheels passing over the wrong tongue of facing points. It took the form of wedges which held the blade tight against the stock rail, the sliding type wedges being operated by the respective signals.

In 1867/8, Livesey, Edwards and Jeffreys patented a point lock which was a 12 foot long bar, laid close to the approach rails and balanced like a bevelled ruler. To move the blades, the bar had to be raised but this was impossible if vehicles were resting on the bar. Originally operated by the same lever as the points, the arrangement was amended in 1869 by Saxby & Farmer to a separate locking apparatus

lever, which gave the signalman visible indication by lever position as to whether the points were locked or free.

The locking bar came in 1870 as a bolt acting on a bar between the blades placed so that the bolt would not go fully 'home' in the bar until the points were properly set. The locking bolt did not differentiate if the points had moved in response to the lever, but 'backlocking' with the signal prevented an erroneous indication.

Stevens introduced a device in 1871 without lock bolt but with a bar which lay beside the rail and could be moved away either by the signal or wheel flange. Thus, when a wheel flange was between bar and rail, a signal could not be restored to Danger. In effect a signal 'backlock', with the signal lever locking the point lever which could not be moved. The bar was counterbalanced to return against the rail after the passage of a train.

Basic principles of these early devices remain to this day, and although many other patents were to be taken out, the basic objectives, of holding points securely in the correct position for each route and giving a correct signal indication only after points were correctly set and proved, were present.

The Board of Trade were, however, reluctant to give too free a rein to facing point locks and the words, ". . . facing points to be avoided as far as possible . . ." continued to

Plate 133: Point operating mechanisms at Quainton Road Junction, on the Great Central Railway, electrically worked from a 20 volt machine, 721 yards from the signal box at Quainton Road Station.   *Author's Collection*

Plate 134: Facing point locking mechanism operated by a rod from the top right. Note the two slots in the tie bar for blade locking in either 'normal' or 'reversed' positions.

Author

appear in their regulations until 1907. The maximum distance from lever to point in 1874 was 120 yards, raised in 1877 to 150 yards, and following the introduction of travelling rollers for point rodding in 1885, to 180 yards. In 1900, the distance was increased to 200 yards and if the facing point lock was detected as well as the blades, this became 250 yards in 1905, with provision for extension to 300 yards if the points were power operated. This dual condition lasted until 1925 when the limit was raised to 350 yards if mechanically-operated, or indefinitely if power-operated.

However, in November 1921, the GC operated a main line double junction 721 yards from the signal box at Quainton Road, operation being by 20 volt machine, with no locking bar. Track circuits controlled the signalling, the signals detecting the point electrically. The point mechanism is shown in **Plate 133**.

One example of facing point locking is shown in **Plate 134**, a typical treadle depression bar being in **Plate 135**. Two GER arrangements are depicted in **Figures 51 & 52** (overleaf).

Plate 135: A treadle bar, depressed by a vehicle tyre, causing locking to be held at the point blades. In some cases, the treadle was used as a train detector, working with track circuits and the signal box illuminated diagram.

Author

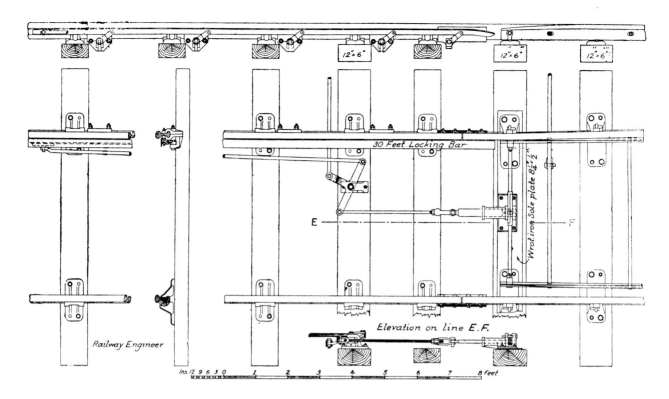

Figure 51: A facing point lock with a 30ft. locking bar, as used on the Great Eastern Railway, the length of the bar being longer than the maximum space between vehicle wheelsets. The F.P.L. connection to the signal lever passes at right angles under the rail from the 'T' crank. When the lock was inserted in the point tie bar, the locking bar moved to the left in an arc which took it level with the rail top in its travel. If the rail section was occupied subsequently by a vehicle, the wheel flange prevented the bar rising in an unlocking arc, the points remaining locked. Signals could not be lowered until the points were locked. In the diagram above, the point is shown unlocked.

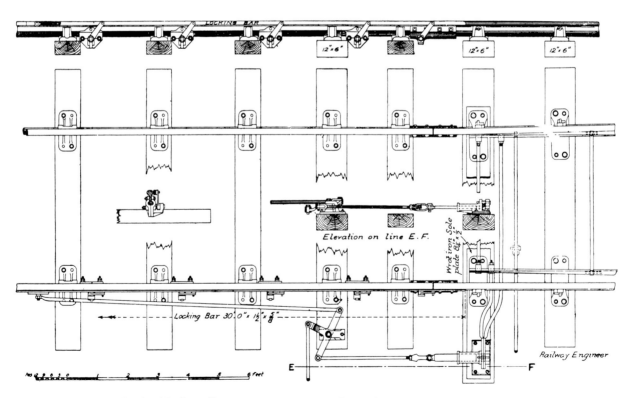

Figure 52: The locking bar in this Great Eastern arrangement was located outside the running rail and thus functioned with the wheel tread, not the flange. In other respects, its operation was similar to that in **Figure 51**, but being outside the track, conventional direct lever locking on the rail centre line was facilitated.

Slotting of Signals

A signal arm which is fitted with a device to prevent it moving from its most restrictive aspect until a control has been operated from two or more separate lever frames is said to be 'slotted'. The control device for the arm is in most circumstances, fitted to the signal balance weights, but this arrangement does not prevent the signal being restored to normal by any one of the controls. Distant signals are the type most frequently 'slotted' and are generally worked from the signal box (or ground frame) in rear, but the signal arm does not respond to the lever until the control from the signal box or ground frame in advance is operated. The device is also employed to ensure full braking distance and also in conjunction with level crossings. The Home signal at an advance signal box may also be 'slotted' to act as the Starting signal from the box in rear on short sections to provide for safer working.

In respect of braking distances, the provision of a Distant signal arm on the same post as a Home signal may not guarantee adequate braking distance, and in these circumstances, an additional or 'outer Distant' will be provided beneath the next rear Stop signal or independently, both Distant arms being simultaneously slotted.

In most instances, as in the GC example in **Figure 54**, or the more customary 'drop off slot' illustrated in **Figure 53**, slotting is attained by plates attached to the balance weight arms. However, on the Great Northern, a wire arrangement was used located away from the signal post, as in **Figure 55**.

In operation, the balance weight nearest the post is connected to the Home signal and also the lever frame. The centre arm is connected to the Distant signal arm only, and the outer balance weight arm is connected to the lever of the box in advance, but not to a signal arm. Clearance of the Home signal leaves the centre arm clear to move by gravity when the Distant lever is pulled at the box in advance, but when the Home signal is replaced to danger, the cross piece on the centre arm is also raised, restoring the Distant signal to Caution. Replacement of the Distant lever can be done subsequently by the signalman at the advance box. In the event of the Distant lever being erroneously pulled, the arm will not clear as the crosspiece on the centre arm is held by the Home signal arm balance weight. If the box in advance is closed, such as for long section working, and all signal levers are pulled each time the man in rear clears his Home signal, the Distant arm will also clear. Obviously any balance weight attached to the centre arm must be less than the weight of either of the lever-controlled balance weight arms.

Signal slotting is depicted in **Plates 136 & 137**.

Figure 53: The conventional 'drop-off' slot arrangement, which could be used either with a 'stop' and 'distant' common post signal, or to control one signal arm controlled by two signal boxes in short section working, or by a combination of a ground frame and a signal box.

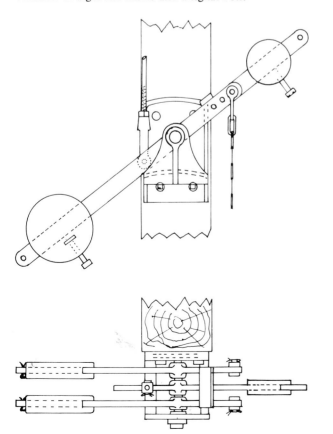

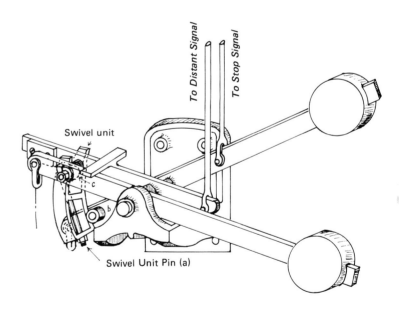

Figure 54: Great Central Railway 'slotting' arrangements. The arm mounted in the centre of the unit and attached to the Distant, or controlled signal arm, had mounted upon it a swivel unit operating on the pin (a). Two rollers, marked (b) and (c), on the Home and controlled unit arms, travelled down the swivel unit. Whichever signal lever was pulled first, forced the appropriate roller down the swivel unit and also 'locked' the other roller, so that when the signal lever was pulled, the centre arm moved down with it, thus 'clearing' that main signal arm. In the diagram, the Home signal lever has been pulled thus 'locking' the centre arm in such a way that when the Distant signal lever is pulled, the centre arm will also move and clear that signal.

Plate 136: An example of a single arm lattice post slot arrangement at Dundee. The weight marked 'LNER 40', nearest to the camera, is linked to the lever in a ground frame, the other left hand one being linked to a signal box. Both are fitted with detection equipment (right lower). The signal arm is connected to the right hand balance weight, and with the '⊥' shape bar adjacent to the pivot, the arm cannot be cleared until both signal levers are pulled. In the illustration, only the 'slot' is pulled (LNER 40) and the arm is restrained until the other (signal) lever is pulled. Conversely, replacement of either 'slot' or 'signal' lever will place the signal to 'stop' by forcing up the signal balance weight, it being lighter.

Author

Plate 137: Signal slotting on the Great Northern Railway signal at the National Railway Museum. The balance weight, nearer the post, was linked to both signal and lever frame, the centre one to the Distant signal only, the outer being only to the lever for the Distant signal. The 'L' shaped iron plate bridged all three balance weight arms. When the Home was pulled, the signal cleared normally, leaving the gravitational effect of the centre arm clear to move when the Distant lever was pulled. When the Home was restored, the 'L' plate also was forced upwards, thus restoring the Distant arm to Caution, restoration of the signal lever subsequently locking it in position. Note the use of rods linking the balance weights to the signal arms and the threaded adjusters. These rods pushed the arms into the 'clear' position, and are mounted on the opposite side of a common pivot to the upper quadrant arrangement as shown in **Plate 136**.

Author

Most signal slotting arrangements were fitted to signal posts where the signal arm balance weights and counter-balance could be readily grouped together, but on the Great Northern Railway, inter alia, a slotting arrangement was used which was remote from the signal post, being located 'in advance' of the Home signal, although conventional arm balance weights were on the post. The Great Northern arrangement is shown in **Figure 55**.

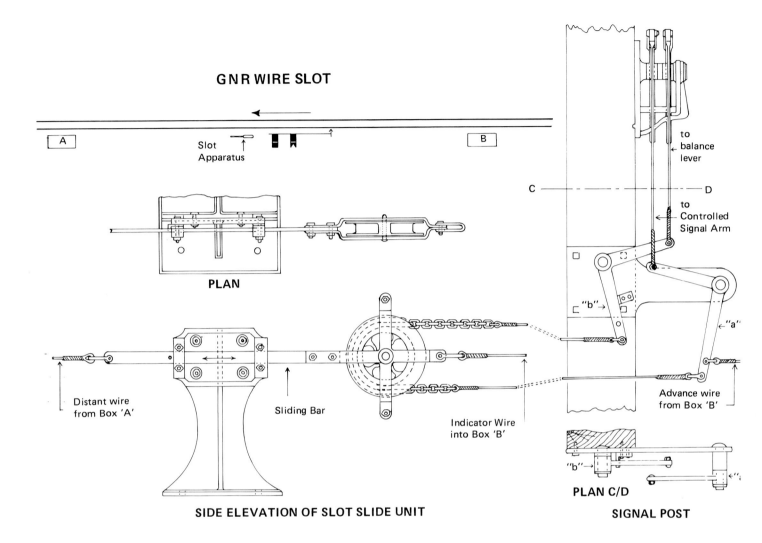

GNR WIRE SLOT

Slot Apparatus

A

B

PLAN

SIDE ELEVATION OF SLOT SLIDE UNIT

Distant wire from Box 'A'

Sliding Bar

Indicator Wire into Box 'B'

to balance lever

C ———— D

to Controlled Signal Arm

"b"→

←"a"

Advance wire from Box 'B'

PLAN C/D

SIGNAL POST

Figure 55: 'A' and 'B' are two signal boxes. The 'stop' signal is under the direct control of the signalman at 'B', by conventional wires to the signal lever, the distant signal arm mounted on the same post but below the 'stop' arm relating to 'stop' signals under the control of the signalman at 'A'. The distant signal arm cannot be cleared until the 'stop' signal arm, above, is lowered, and when the latter is replaced to 'danger', the distant signal arm is required to revert to 'caution' simultaneously. Crank (a) at the base of the signal post was linked to the 'stop' signal arm, crank (b) being linked to the distant arm and by a wire and chain arrangement around a pulley, which was normally slack, to crank (a). The lever in 'A', for operating the distant arm, was linked to the sliding bar and the pulley wheel, with an extension to an instrument in box 'B', to show the lever position, but not to the distant arm or crank. When the signalman at 'B' pulled his home signal lever, the signal arm duly responded, this action also tightening the loose wire and chain around the pulley. When the distant signal lever was pulled with the 'stop' signal cleared, the slide moved to the left, taking with it the pulley, and as the wire round it was anchored to crank (a), the end attached to crank (b) pulled that crank towards the slide and lowered the arm. When the 'stop' signal was replaced to danger, crank (a) moved towards the slide and detensioned the cable round the pulley, enabling the arm balance weight for the distant arm to place the arm to 'caution', irrespective of the lever position in box 'A'. Replacement of the lever at 'A' merely further slackened the wire between cranks (a) and (b). If the distant lever had been pulled, or left over, when the 'stop' signal arm was at 'danger', only the initial tensioning would occur which would not be sufficient to operate the arm.

Chapter Four

Mechanical Interlocking

Mechanical Interlocking

Interlocking is defined as 'a means of ensuring that point, signal, etc., levers are in correct positions before a signal can be cleared and that the route set up is maintained and levers controlling conflicting movements are prevented from being operated until the lever concerned is restored to the normal position.

In 1843, Sir Charles Gregory, of semaphore signal fame, gathered the operating chains of eight signals at Bricklayers Arms into a foot-operated stirrup type frame which was equipped with mechanical linkage that prevented conflicting signals indication. On the same platform as the frame were six point levers which were neither interlocked with each other or with the signals.

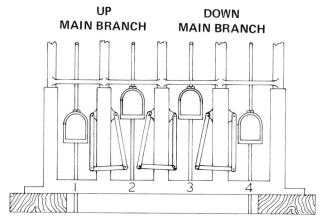

Figure 56: A typical Gregory type signal frame, with stirrup locking arrangement. See Figure 57 for signal plan.

Figure 58: A Chambers development of a Gregory frame (right). Point interlocking is incorporated and this figure should also be read in conjunction with Figure 57.

Various devices were developed to interlock signals and points, but most achieved only limited effect and usually locked one signal with one pair of points, performing more of a 'slotting' action until in 1856 Saxby introduced a signal interlocking frame in which no conflicting signal to point setting could be given, by linking both signal and point connections to the same lever.

The opening of the Hampstead Junction line in October, 1859 was delayed until the signalling installation satisfied the Board of Trade Inspector. The contractors, Messrs. Stevens & Sons tried, but failed, and it was one of the railway employees, Austin Chambers who eventually devised a satisfactory arrangement. In an essentially 'Gregory' frame, the principle of stirrup and point lever was retained, but the lever was fitted with a plate drilled to accept the pin at the base of the stirrup. When a point lever was set for a route, the signal stirrup could be depressed as the pin could pass through the hole. Movement of the point lever put hole and stirrup pin out of alignment and the signal could not be lowered. When the signal could be cleared, the point lever could not be reversed as it was held by the stirrup pin. The Inspector approved the apparatus and Chambers received a cheque from his employers to patent the arrangement. A few weeks later the patent was offered to Stevens, but refused, the price asked being £100. Chambers locking did not cover Distant signals.

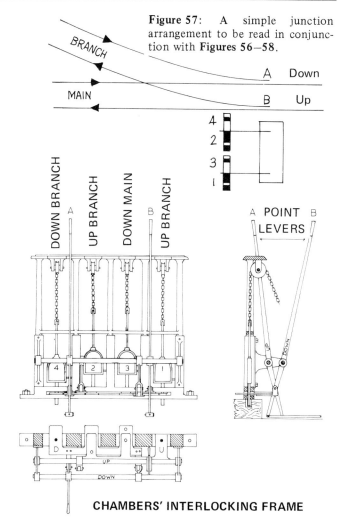

Figure 57: A simple junction arrangement to be read in conjunction with Figures 56—58.

CHAMBERS' INTERLOCKING FRAME

A variation of the Chambers apparatus was found where the signal was operated by a lever with an arc-shaped extension on the rear which locked the lever plate in a similar manner to the stirrup. This replacement of stirrup by lever paved the way for larger lever frames, and with this came great improvements in interlocking arrangements.

The first major step came from Stevens with 'hook interlocking' (Figure 59). A spiral spring pressed bars to the left, movement to the right being by lever pressure against angled portions of locking plates. Lever catches 'back-locked' points by signals.

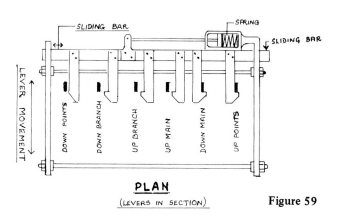

PLAN
(LEVERS IN SECTION)

Figure 59

Saxby & Farmer 'hook locking' (**Figure 60**) was achieved by using pivoted locking bars, thus dispensing with springs.

Many varieties of interlocking arrangements were designed and patented, each working on the general principle of horizontally moving lock bars and vertical moving levers. Each patentee jealously guarded their invention, often going to litigation when infringement was suspected, one notable case, between Saxby & Farmer and McKenzie & Holland lasting for four years and going as far as the House of Lords.

In 1870, Stevens took out a patent for an invention called 'tappet interlocking', invented by James Deakin, one of their employees. Unfortunately, they forgot to renew their patent fee in 1885 and the system became public property. Many signalling firms (and railway companies) adopted the system and although some modifications were made, the basic principle remained. A typical example of tappet interlocking appears in the diagram of Wisbech St. Mary in **Figure 61** albeit simplified to omit spare levers.

Initially, lever movement activated the locking. The lever had to be moved a certain distance before other levers became locked and slackness in the apparatus could have enabled a signalman to lower an unauthorized signal. In the Easterbrook system, the locking in the frame locked the lever catch handle preventing its release and in 1888 Saxby & Farmer abandoned tumbler locking for tappet interlocking where the lever catch operated the locking in the frame. In addition to thus relieving the locking of some 80 per cent of the strain caused by lever locking, a wrong signal could not be given either by negligence, or strain or slackness in the locking apparatus, as before the lever could be moved, the catch handle had to be worked. The resultant frame was known as the Saxby & Farmer Patent Duplex Locking Frame.

By 1873, 37 per cent of all signals were concentrated, 40 per cent were interlocked and safety points provided at 40 per cent of goods line junctions and siding connections. Following the unsuccessful endeavour to promote a Bill which sought Block system adoption and concentration and interlocking of points and signals within five years, the Railway Regulation Act of 1873 was passed which ordered progress monitoring in respect of passenger lines.

Between 1873 and 1889, locking of Starting signals with Block instruments had been progressed, predominantly under the influence of W. R. Sykes, his famous 'Lock and Block', which is dealt with later, being installed on a number of lines.

The Regulation of Railways Act, 1889, ordered that all points and signals be concentrated and interlocked within two years. At that time, however, some 90 per cent of connections had been interlocked, which by 1895 stood at 95 per cent.

By the turn of the century, mechanical interlocking was at its zenith and frame size had increased in the larger installations to a degree that was physically exhausting to their unfortunate signalmen. The mechanical frame at Newcastle No. 1 had some 244 levers, Edinburgh Waverley having no less than 260, the largest single frame at the time in Great Britain until supplanted by York Locomotive Yard box in 1907.

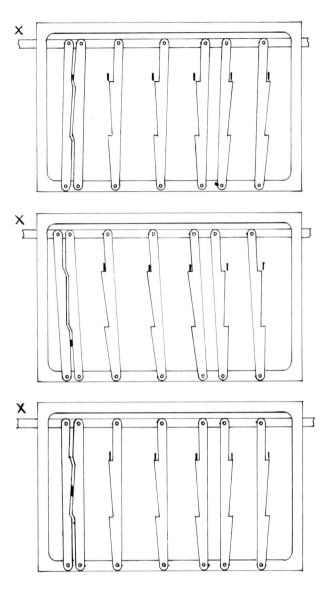

Figure 60: Early Saxby & Farmer locking frame arrangement. In this equipment, the Stevens' 'hook locking' principle is retained but the spring is replaced by a sliding bar (X) activated by the 'down' points lever. In the centre position, all points and signals are locked. Other letters and numbers relate to **Figure 57**.

The time was therefore ripe for developing power assisted lever frames, which by relieving the signalman of much physical effort, enabled more of their attention to be given to train controlling purposes.

Examples of mechanical locking frames are depicted in **Plates 138–153**, and in **Figures 63 & 64**.

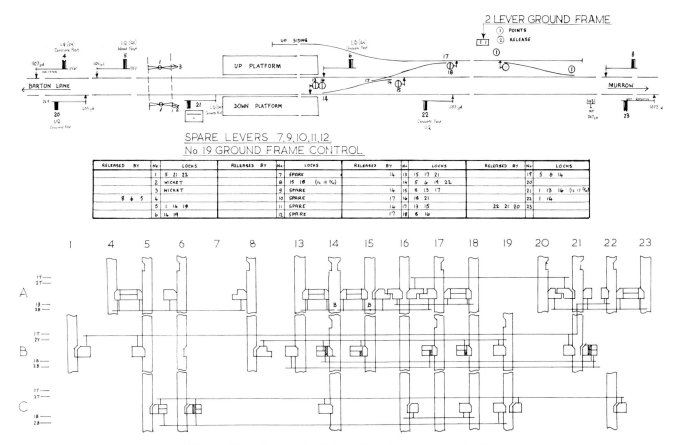

2 LEVER GROUND FRAME
① POINTS
② RELEASE

SPARE LEVERS 7,9,10,11,12
No 19 GROUND FRAME CONTROL.

RELEASED BY	No	LOCKS	RELEASED BY	No	LOCKS	RELEASED BY	No	LOCKS	RELEASED BY	No	LOCKS
	1	5 21 22		7	SPARE	14	13	15 17 21		19	5 6 14
	2	WICKET		8	15 18 (14 19 ‰)		14	5 6 19 22		20	
	3	WICKET		9	SPARE	14	15	8 13 17		21	1 13 16 (14 17 ‰)
8 6 5	4			10	SPARE	17	16	14 21		22	1 14
	5	1 14 19		11	SPARE	14	17	13 15	22 21 20	23	
	6	14 19		12	SPARE	17	18	8 16			

Figure 61: Track, 'pull board' and tappet interlocking arrangement at Wisbech St. Mary (M&GNJR).

Signal box locking is of two types, mechanical, where the lever controls another in the same frame, and electrical, mostly achieved by devices such as track circuits, point detention apparatus, etc., outside the box, although the actual locking gear is located either below the operating floor or behind the frame inside the box.

Each lever has a catch handle which must be activated before the lever can be moved. In most mechanical frames, locking controls the catch handle as well as the lever.

Levers have two extreme positions, 'normal', where it stands away from the signalman or 'back in the frame' to use railway terminology, as in **Figure 62(a)**. Where levers are electrically 'backlocked', the lever has an intermediate position, known as 'on the backlock', as in **Figure 62(c)**.

When levers are 'normal', signals display their most restrictive aspect. Front locking prevents signal clearance unless certain safety considerations permit. After lever reversal, the backlock would hold it in that position, although if electrical locking was used, the lever could be placed 'on the backlock', which would enable the signal to be replaced but would not affect locking on other levers interlocked with it as the full lever stroke was not made. As an example, a Distant signal is front-locked until the Home signal(s) is pulled, the Home(s) being backlocked until the Distant lever is replaced to 'normal'. In electrical interlocking, a Home signal would be held at Danger after lever replacement by the action of a track circuit between Home and Starter. Where Sykes 'Lock and Block' is operative, after Home or Starter had been cleared, it could be replaced

Figure 62: Lever positions in a mechanical frame showing (a) normal, (b) reversed and (c) lever 'on the backlock'. The functions of the positions are set out in the adjoining text.

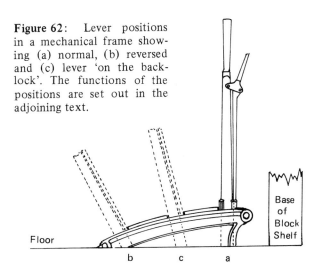

to Danger by placing the appropriate lever into the position of **Figure 62(c)** but it cannot be placed fully 'normal' until electrical clearance has been given by a train passing over a rail contact in advance of the signal.

A signalman can, by consulting his frame layout, determine when a mechanical front or backlock can be replaced, electrical locking being almost invariably indicated by instruments on the block shelf.

Plate 138: The Cairntows signal box at Duddingston, near Edinburgh, was fitted with a Stevens 9 lever ground frame. **(See Plate 316).**

Author

Plate 139: A section of the conventional Stevens pattern lever frame, at Markinch, Fife. A 'collar' hangs on the block shelf support and a detonator placer stirrup is on the frame between levers 5 and 6. The painted numbers on the levers relate to the sequence required before the levers can be reversed.

Author

Plate 140: The Stevens 25 lever frame at Gorebridge, on the North British 'Waverley Route'. The block shelf above the levers contains original NBR block instruments (left) and bells. The right hand instrument is of BR origin combining 'up' and 'down' lines in one case. The equipment at the extreme right is a lamp indicator, electrically worked, which warns of signal lamp extinguishment.

W. S. Sellar

Plate 141: Saxby & Farmer were the main signalling contractors for the West Highland Railway when it opened in 1894, and they installed the above signal frame in the platform signal box at Arrochar & Tarbet. Distant signals for both 'up' and 'down' lines are equipped with wheel type wire tensioning gear and these can be seen behind the levers.

Author

Plate 142: The small mechanical frame at Cargo Fleet Station Old Crossing, North Eastern Railway, the outside levers of which were worked by turning the small side-mounted wheels.

R. Preston

Plate 143: The McKenzie & Holland mechanical locking frame at Brampton Fell, North Eastern Railway, with the original lever board behind the frame. Note the double quadrant rails at each lever.

R. Preston

Plate 144: The McKenzie & Holland frame at Oak Tree, between Darlington and Middlesbrough, with single lever quadrant rails. Signal repeater and track circuit indicators are mounted on the front of the block shelf. The numbers on the side of the levers give the sequence of 'pulls' required before the lever concerned can be released from its locking.

R. Preston

Plate 145: Long Beck interlocking frame, near Saltburn, incorporating tensioning handles for the Distant signals and a crossing gate operating wheel of maritime design. Note also the 'stirrup' gear for the Home signals (6 and 7) and the unusual pivot arrangement for lever No. 2. The stirrups were used for the mechanical positioning of detonators on the rails.

R. Preston

Plate 146: Guisborough Junction box, near Middlesbrough, was equipped with a 140 lever McKenzie & Holland frame, although latterly, many became spare and painted white as a need for their use ceased. North Eastern instruments are on the block shelf.

N. D. Mundy

Plate 147: A Duttons frame was fitted at the Clipstone East signal box by the Great Central Railway.

N. D. Mundy

Plate 148: A scaled down version of a North Eastern Railway locking frame, with full mechanical interlocking, formed part of the equipment provided by the LNER as part of a Signalling Training School, established at York. The frame was part of a model railway layout and was, of course, fully signalled with miniatures of North Eastern lower quadrant signals, and provided staff dealing with the construction and maintenance of signals, telegraph and telephone installations instructions, with principles of electrical and mechanical signalling and telegraphy and telephony. Operating staff were also trained in Rules and Regulations of train and traffic working.

LNER

Plate 149: The school also included full size equipment for practical experience away from actual day to day operations, and ▶ the example illustrated on the opposite page, is a 5 lever interlocking frame with lever electrical contact boxes.

LNER

FIVE LEVER
INTERLOCKING FRAME
FULL SIZE

LEVER
CONTACT BOXES

Plate 150: The 260 lever continuous interlocking frame at Edinburgh Waverley East installed by the Railway Signal Company, Fazakerley. At the time of installation, it was the longest continuous frame in the world.

Author's Collection

Plate 151: The 244 lever mechanical locking frame, at Newcastle No. 1 signal box, before the installation of electro-pneumatic signalling.

Author's Collection

Plate 152: Back to back lever frames, installed by McKenzie & Holland, in one of the Liverpool Street signal boxes.

Plate 153: The largest single unit mechanical locking frame in Great Britain, of 295 levers, installed in York Locomotive Yard signal box.

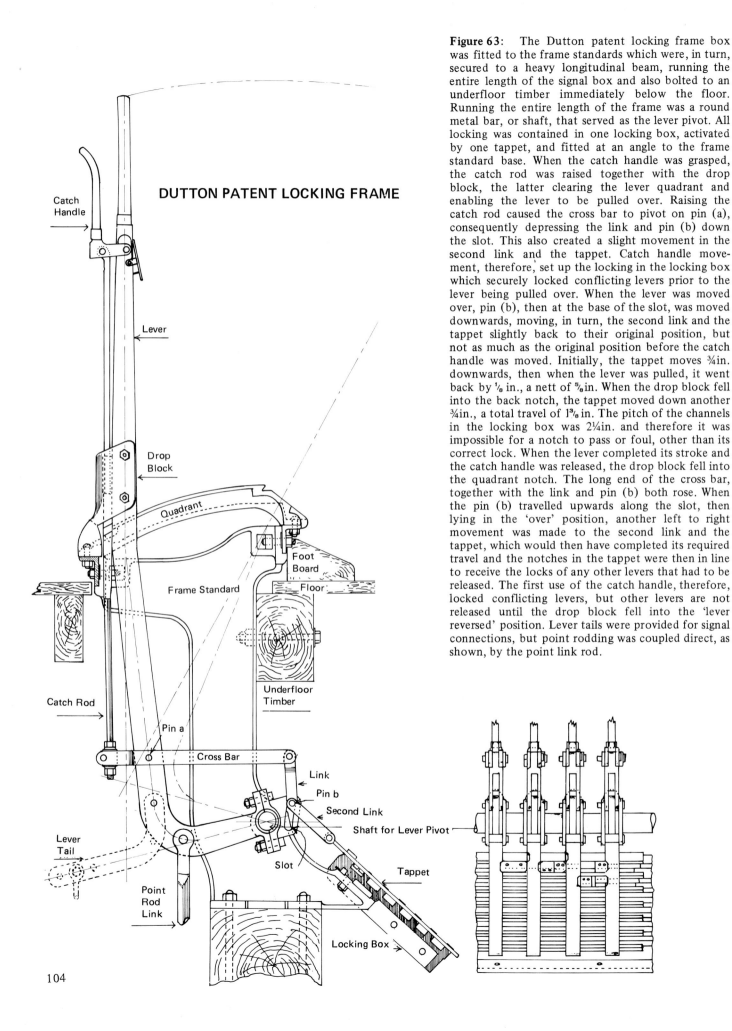

DUTTON PATENT LOCKING FRAME

Catch
Handle

Lever

Drop
Block

Quadrant

Foot
Board

Floor

Frame Standard

Underfloor
Timber

Catch Rod

Pin a

Cross Bar

Link

Pin b

Second Link

Lever
Tail

Shaft for Lever Pivot

Slot

Tappet

Point
Rod
Link

Locking Box

Figure 63: The Dutton patent locking frame box was fitted to the frame standards which were, in turn, secured to a heavy longitudinal beam, running the entire length of the signal box and also bolted to an underfloor timber immediately below the floor. Running the entire length of the frame was a round metal bar, or shaft, that served as the lever pivot. All locking was contained in one locking box, activated by one tappet, and fitted at an angle to the frame standard base. When the catch handle was grasped, the catch rod was raised together with the drop block, the latter clearing the lever quadrant and enabling the lever to be pulled over. Raising the catch rod caused the cross bar to pivot on pin (a), consequently depressing the link and pin (b) down the slot. This also created a slight movement in the second link and the tappet. Catch handle movement, therefore, set up the locking in the locking box which securely locked conflicting levers prior to the lever being pulled over. When the lever was moved over, pin (b), then at the base of the slot, was moved downwards, moving, in turn, the second link and the tappet slightly back to their original position, but not as much as the original position before the catch handle was moved. Initially, the tappet moves ¾in. downwards, then when the lever was pulled, it went back by ⅛ in., a nett of ⅝in. When the drop block fell into the back notch, the tappet moved down another ¾in., a total travel of 1⅜in. The pitch of the channels in the locking box was 2¼in. and therefore it was impossible for a notch to pass or foul, other than its correct lock. When the lever completed its stroke and the catch handle was released, the drop block fell into the quadrant notch. The long end of the cross bar, together with the link and pin (b) both rose. When the pin (b) travelled upwards along the slot, then lying in the 'over' position, another left to right movement was made to the second link and the tappet, which would then have completed its required travel and the notches in the tappet were then in line to receive the locks of any other levers that had to be released. The first use of the catch handle, therefore, locked conflicting levers, but other levers are not released until the drop block fell into the 'lever reversed' position. Lever tails were provided for signal connections, but point rodding was coupled direct, as shown, by the point link rod.

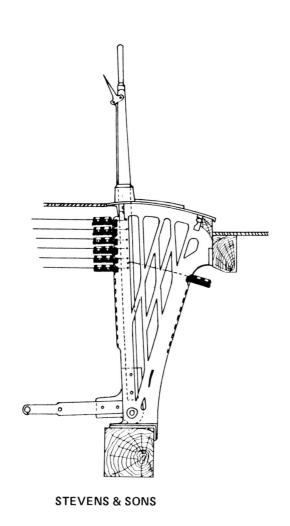

STEVENS & SONS

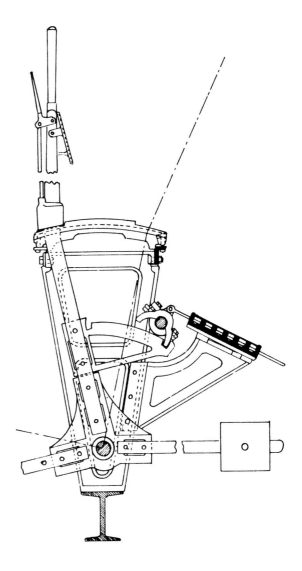

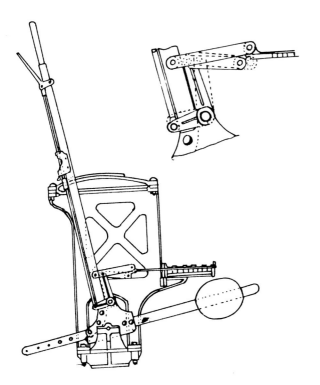

Figure 64: In 1923, the London & North Eastern Railway had in use the greatest variety of lever frames of the 'Big Four'. There were, in fact, some 28 variations of the McKenzie & Holland type alone, not counting the various evolutions of other signalling contractors and railway company designs. It would, therefore, be difficult to give each the detailed treatment given to the Dutton pattern in **Figure 63**, and, therefore, further diagrams on lever frames are confined to the three on this page. Stevens' pattern frames were common north of the border as were the Saxby & Farmer patent Duplex types on the Great Northern after their introduction in 1888. The Evans–O'Donnell type was also produced as a 'catch handle' locking frame, but the lever locking occupied less operating space.

Chapter Five

Power Interlocking and Signalling

Power Interlocking and Signalling

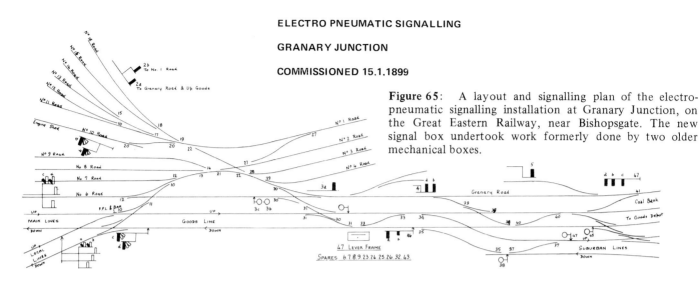

ELECTRO PNEUMATIC SIGNALLING

GRANARY JUNCTION

COMMISSIONED 15.1.1899

Figure 65: A layout and signalling plan of the electro-pneumatic signalling installation at Granary Junction, on the Great Eastern Railway, near Bishopsgate. The new signal box undertook work formerly done by two older mechanical boxes.

The first electro-pneumatic installation in Britain was at Granary Junction, near Bishopsgate, on the Great Eastern which was commissioned in January 1899. The locking frame, which was of similar construction to those used in America, comprised 11 levers for 21 signals and 4 slots; 26 levers for 43 points and 3 locking bars, and 10 spare levers. All 47 levers were contained in a length of 10 feet 8 inches, a very considerable space economy. If normal mechanical locking had been used, it was reckoned that two signal boxes would have been required. An animated diagram was supplied by which the signalman could identify the lie of points by small flags moving with the lever. A line diagram of the installation is in **Figure 65**. The new signal box displaced two older cabins.

In 1902, the North Eastern installed E.P. locking on the Tyne Dock approaches, as at Granary on a freight only line. It was later extended to cover other lines in the Tyne Dock area with five frames covering 114 points and 173 signals by 164 levers. The main signalling contractors for the scheme were Messrs. McKenzie & Holland Limited, who were agents for the 'Westinghouse' electro-pneumatic system. The signals followed conventional North Eastern Railway lower quadrant 'slotted' post practice, the E.P. valves being placed on the signal post or 'doll' below the arms they operated.

Signal boxes in the Tyne Dock scheme, which was not completed until June 1905, were at Pledworth Lane, Pontop Crossing, Tyne Dock (Green Lane), Bank Top and Tyne Dock Bottom. In addition to the normal operation of points and signals, level crossing gate operation was in a similar manner to the points, using small levers to control valves for gates and gate stops. The gate motor was larger than usual to counteract strong winds, but the gate lever controlled a graduating valve provided to suit prevailing wind strength. The gate movement could be quickly stopped, or reversed, if required.

One of the signal boxes, shortly after commissioning, is depicted in **Plate 154**, together with the signal bridge upon which is mounted a smaller signal bridge with main line arms. All signal arms in the illustration are endorsed with the line of route, to which they refer, and the use of a Distant signal arm, in advance of the crossover in lieu of a Home, is interesting.

Plate 154: Pontop Crossing, where the goods lines from Tyne Dock cross, on the level, the Gateshead to Sunderland passenger line. In later years, the signal box was doubled in length, and track and signalling rationalization was implemented which eliminiated the crossover, in the foreground, and all the visible signal gantries, these being replaced, where required, by bracket signals.

Author's Collection

Plate 155: A Crewe type all electric locking frame, at Severus Junction, York, installed in 1903 by the North Eastern Railway. This was the only British example outside the London & North Western Railway and was located at the north end of York yard where all lines worked were for freight traffic, there being no passenger line connections. Note the alternate lever placings in the two rows.

LNER

Plate 156: Tappet interlocking in the conventional manner was provided in the six long horizontal locking boxes underneath the operating floor of the signal box. The locking was actuated by 'bell crank' or 'T' levers, one arm of which was coupled to the lever down rod and the other to the locking bars in the boxes. Below the locking boxes were switches, and under these, the check locks.

LNER

Plate 157: The exterior of Severus Junction signal box which was of standard North Eastern Railway brick and timber construction type. Note the presence of the oil lamp on the right hand end, although the box was electrically lit and note too the standard white oval, edged in black, over the nameboard, which indicates that all signalling equipment was in order.

LNER

In the autumn of 1903, the NER commissioned the Railway Signal Company to instal a large 'Crewe' type signalling plant at Severus Junction, York, at the north end of York Yard, and controlling the arrival and departure line and extensive marshalling sidings which had then been recently extended and remodelled. All lines worked by the signal box were freight only, there being no passenger line connections.

The frame took its name from nine similar frames installed in the Crewe area, on the LNWR, of varying sizes, four other such frames being located at Euston (2) and Camden (2).

The Severus Junction installation was of 133 levers, made up of 101 working and 32 spares, arranged in two tiers at alternate lever spacings (Plate 155). From the levers, down rods passed through the operating floor, under which they were connected to a conventional form of mechanical tappet interlocking before the electrical equipment was reached (Plate 156). If a purely mechanical frame had been used, with levers at 5 inch centres, a frame length of some 55 feet 10 inches would have been required, but the use of the 'Crewe' system enabled this to be restricted to only 21 feet 10½ inches; a very substantial space economy.

The actual signal box, which was 28 feet 4½ inches long inside, was of conventional North Eastern Railway (Southern Division) architectural pattern, as shown in Plate 157.

The first LNER constituent passenger line electro-pneumatic installation was at Hull Paragon where two signal boxes were built containing 159 and 179 lever frames respectively, one being illustrated in Plate 158.

North Eastern signalling practice decreed that if a main line signal was to be cleared, the 'calling on' arm preceding it also had to be cleared, if provided. Increasing mechanical frame sizes meant that a fair amount of walking was involved, and as the distance from boxes to points increased, so did the effort required to pull the levers.

The Newcastle Central area resignalling for the opening of the King Edward Bridge was by McKenzie & Holland and was to E.P. principles. Two views of the signals at the station are given in Plates 159 & 160. 'Calling on' and main line arms were both worked by one lever, the first half of the movement clearing the former, a full stroke clearing the latter. Certain signals and facing points were linked to two levers, either of which would operate them, to save time in bi-directional working by allocating a lever in the order of signals from either direction. The full scheme involved 10 lever frames, with 938 levers of four inch length at two and three quarter inches pitch. Track circuits were used which controlled signals and an illuminated diagram. Lever frame operated train describers were also provided. Other Newcastle signals are shown in Plates 161 & 162.

Plate 158: The exterior of one of the signal boxes, built at Hull Paragon in 1905, for the electro-pneumatic signalling scheme, which survived until the resignalling of Hull Paragon in 1938.

LNER

Plate 159: The gantry-mounted signal box, at the east end of Newcastle Central, with electro-pneumatic operated signalling.
Courtesy National Railway Museum

Plate 160: Signalling at the west end of Newcastle Central, looking west, with Newcastle No. 3 box in the background.
LNER

Plate 161: In addition to covering the main lines in the vicinity of Newcastle Central Station, the E.P. signalling scheme also encompassed lines to the south of the Tyne, extending eastwards to Park Lane Junction on the Sunderland line. The signal box, and some signals which it operated, are depicted above, in this view looking west.

LNER

Plate 162: Park Lane Junction signalling, looking eastwards.

LNER

Whilst the Newcastle installation was in progress, the Great Central commissioned the Ardwick to Newton widening in May 1905 which incorporated low pressure pneumatic signalling over the 6 miles. Notwithstanding additional trackwork, 20 mechanical signal boxes were replaced by 14, with a total lever reduction from 727 to 425. Power came from a building containing three vertical boilers and two compressors near Guide Bridge East box **(Plate 163)**. A main pipe carried dried compressed air to all signal boxes where the pressure was reduced from 40 to 15 p.s.i., the working pressure. The compressed air was stored in large tanks near signal boxes, whence it was supplied to all point and signal mechanisms.

Air pressure at 7 p.s.i. was used to operate the relay valves which admitted air to the mechanisms.

Plate 163: Guide Bridge East signal box of typical Great Central wood construction pattern.

Author

Signal Box	Levers					Signals	Points	Auto Distants
	Signal	Points	Control	Spaces	Total			
Ardwick	21	13	2	4	40	30	24	4
Ashburys East	24	20	–	8	52	37	30	7
Ashburys West	22	14	–	12	48	28	21	–
Priory Junction	28	21	–	15	64	42	37	6
Gorton	21	8	–	7	36	25	14	5
Fairfield	22	11	1	10	44	28	15	6
Fairfield G.F.	3	1	1	3	8	3	2	–
Audenshaw Jct.	12	6	–	6	24	16	10	6
Stockport Jct.	14	15	–	7	36	28	21	12
Stalybridge Jct.	20	19	–	9	48	31	28	11
Guide Bridge Nth.	6	6	–	8	20	10	10	4
Guide Bridge Est.	14	10	–	12	36	18	18	4
Dewsnap	12	7	–	9	28	17	12	–
Hyde Junction	22	15	–	7	44	28	25	3
Newton	12	7	–	5	24	14	7	2
TOTAL	253	173	4	122	552	355	274	70

Figure 66: Tabular summary of the signal boxes and their control responsibilities on the Great Central Railway Ardwick to Newton electro-pneumatic signalling scheme.

The chief advantage of the low pressure system was that problems due to moisture condensation were eliminated and leaks were also less frequent than with a high pressure system.

All operating and indicating pipes were normally subject to atmospheric pressure only, the compressed air being admitted only when points or signals required to be moved.

Check locking was provided on all levers, but movement over the final portion of the stroke was automatic by the air, giving an indication that the motor had responded. Distant signals were worked by the stop signal movement and facing point lock bars by the point levers.

Signal box lever frames had small sliding levers at three inch pitch.

Plate 164: A lower quadrant signal, at Guide Bridge, with steel arms; a later alteration. The operating cylinder is below the Home arm on the lattice post, the route indicator being a later addition. The signals were very similar to the LSWR style.

Author

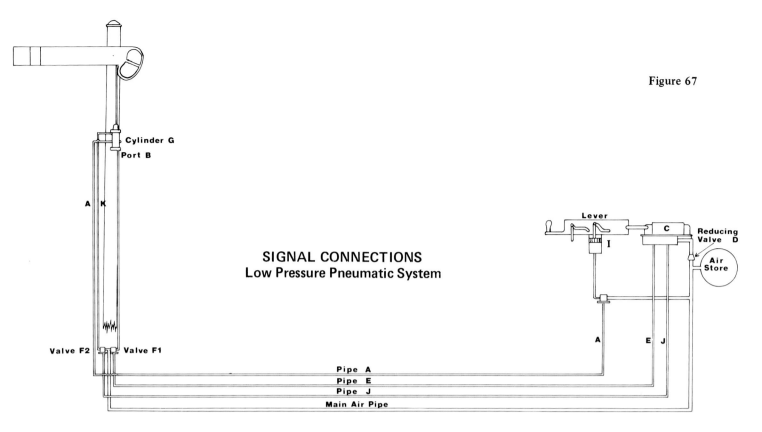

Figure 67

SIGNAL CONNECTIONS
Low Pressure Pneumatic System

Figure 67: The piping and apparatus required to operate a low pressure pneumatic semaphore signal is shown above. The signal box lever is shown in the normal position and pressure is admitted to the upper portion of the signal cylinder by Pipe A and Port B. The lever is then pulled for the full length of its stroke. In so doing, C is moved, admitting air at low pressure from the storage supply, through the reducing valve D to Pipe E which operates Valve F1, supplying air at the high pressure to the lower portion of the Cylinder G, thus forcing up the piston and lowering the signal. When the piston moves, Port B closes. To restore the signal to its most restrictive aspect, the lever is pushed to the right until stopped by the piston rod of H contacting a horizontal slot in the lever. Pipe E is then exhausted, Pipe J is charged and Valve F2 is opened which admits air from the supply through Pipe K to the upper end of Cylinder G, thus restoring the signal.

Figure 68 (below): This shows the pipework required for the operation of pointwork. When the lever is pulled, air is admitted to Pipe E and Valve F1. This in turn admits air at a higher pressure from the main supply source to the left hand end of the Cylinder G, pushing the piston to the right. The points are moved, but the full lever stroke cannot be made until Pipes X and S are connected by Valve Y. Relay Valve H1 is operated and air is admitted to Cylinder J, thereby completing the full stroke automatically. Where it is possible to work more than one signal by a lever, such as a bracket signal at a junction, a selector valve is used and located at the points and worked from the motion plate, similar to the ordinary point indicating valve, except it is fitted with extra ports, the position of the points being the determining factor in signal selection.

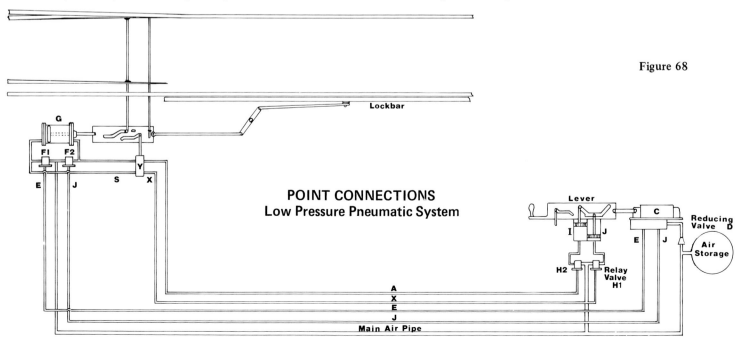

Figure 68

POINT CONNECTIONS
Low Pressure Pneumatic System

Another Great Central low pressure pneumatic scheme was commissioned in 1909 at Wath Concentration Sidings, east of Sheffield, in which four signal boxes were provided, two controlling entry to the sidings, the other two being within the yard. The yard boxes, in addition to having a 12 lever frame, had a push button point operating 'console' with 33 buttons of which 4 were spare. Wath Yard complex had one line fanning out into two 'ladders' with 'king' point selection, the normal lie of which was for the northern ladder. Each point had two vertically-mounted console buttons, the 'normal' lie being achieved by top button depression. The console is shown in **Plate 165 (below)** and above it is the signalling diagram of the 'Wath Gravity Sidings' operated from the unit which was located in cabin 'A'.

Plate 165: The operating console for the low pressure pneumatic point operation undertaken by Wath 'A' box. The action of pressing a button, closed a contact governing the electro-magnetic valve admitting air to the point cylinders. A short track circuit between the point fouling point and signal acted in lieu of facing point locks and bars. Occupation of the track circuits were indicated by a small disc in the console, just above the point control button. When buttons in the top row were pressed, they mechanically moved out the bottom row buttons and vice versa.

Author's Collection

Annett's route indicating signal, which featured a solitary arm and a magazine of routes, each of which was raised into position before an illuminated screen was provided at Elsecar and at Moor Road, the two approach sidings to the Wath Sidings. Normally mechanical, these signals were adapted for E.P. operation and the nine routes available were operated by one lever (which also lowered the arm) instead of the nine which a mechanical arrangement would require. A mechanical version of Annett's signal is depicted in **Plate 70**.

Manchester (London Road) Station was operated jointly by the London & North Western Railway and the Great Central, each having its own portion. When the LNWR widened the lines to Ardwick in 1909, their three new signal boxes were to the 'Crewe' all-electric power system, but the GCR signal box was of the low pressure pneumatic system, being gantry-mounted over the horse-box dock at the end of platform 'C'.

The GCR box was equipped with an 84 lever frame, controlling some 62 points, 29 facing point-lock bars and 58 signals, in its own company territory.

The operation of the points and signals was, as in the Ardwick–Hyde scheme, by compressed air at 15 p.s.i., but a major development was incorporated into the London Road scheme in that the compressed air, after it had performed its work, was not exhausted to the atmosphere, but remained in the pipes and thus held them in either the 'normal' or 'reversed' position. In addition, whereas previously a wrong route could only be reversed after the full point or signal movement had been completed and the lever travelled its full stroke, it was now possible to interrupt the former sequence and effect lever restoration to its original position.

An additional feature was that should a pair of points inadvertently be run through in a trailing position, the piston was forced back into the cylinder and only compressed the air which, when the errant wheels had passed, expanded and restored both points and piston and avoided expensive repairs which would have, otherwise, been necessary in the case of mechanical operation.

The newer method of operation was known as the 'dual pressure system', and was achieved by additional ports being given to the valve of the lever in the locking frame allowing air at low pressure to continually flow in the operating pipes, irrespective of the lever position. This air actuated a valve at the point operating cylinder which admitted air at a high pressure from the main supply which moved the points. It was not possible for air at the low pressure to work the points due to an in-built valve arrangement.

When points required to be reversed, the lever was drawn forward until stopped by the check lock. This put the high pressure supply into the operating pipe to the points which passed into the valve actuating a diaphragm and allowing the low pressure air in the operating cylinder to exhaust to the atmosphere and the higher pressure air moving the piston and thus the point blades.

The ground signals in the scheme were standard BPRS Coy semaphores, as shown in **Plate 117**, but with the operating cylinders fitted to the lower rear of the short 'posts'.

The next development in GCR power signalling took place when the concept of low pressure pneumatic signalling yielded to the direct use of electricity in point and signal operation by adjacent motors, and in 1911 the Great Central introduced Intermediate Block signal to Britain on the Bullwell North–Hucknall–Annesley South Junction route using all-electric Stop and Distant signals, the latter acting as an automatic Stop signal repeater. Tubular posts were used.

The British Pneumatic Railway Signalling Company installed an all-electric signalling scheme at Immingham in 1912, covering both points and signals, as part of work in connection with the development of the deep water port

Plate 166:
An all electric locking frame at Immingham East Junction.

N. D. Mundy

Plate 167: A Great Central bracket signal with main and goods line arms, the latter having the metal 'O' fitted to the arm. At Immingham West, both arms were motor-operated by 'doll'-mounted mechanisms.

P. Tatlow Collection

Plate 168: A three position tubular post upper quadrant signal, of the Great Central Railway, with the arm in the Clear position. The Caution aspect would have the arm at 45 degrees to the horizontal. The signal was one of eight installed at Keadby, in 1916, as a complete scheme, the design being American in origin. The electric operating motor drove direct to the arm spindle, being mounted at arm height. The signal functioned as a semi-automatic.

P. Tatlow Collection

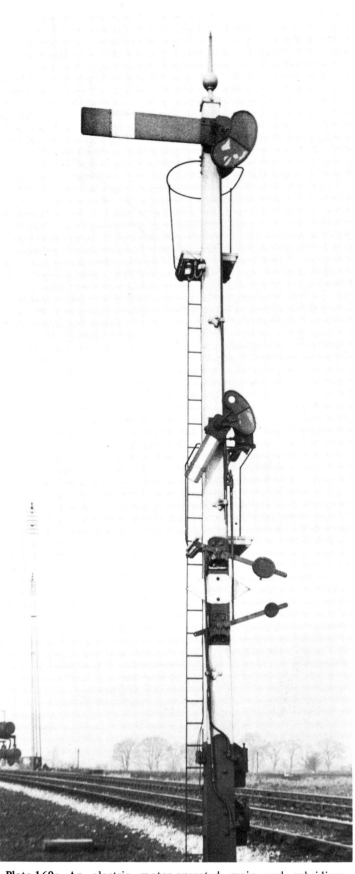

Plate 169: An electric motor-operated main and subsidiary arm, at Keadby Canal. The latter has a white horizontal band on the arm face, and although displaying a normal Clear aspect, when at Danger only a small white light was visible.

P. Tatlow Collection

Plate 170: A rather heavily-braced motor-operated signal, at Keadby Bridge, with electric power lines exposed on the lower portion of the post.

P. Tatlow Collection

which opened on 22nd July 1912. The locking frames, one of which is illustrated in **Plate 166**, were also all-electric. Signals were of conventional GCR lower quadrant type, although electric motor-operated, and an example is depicted in **Plate 167**.

At Keadby, the GCR Doncaster to Scunthorpe line originally crossed the River Trent by a swing bridge which had normal mechanical signalling equipment. When the bridge became life expired, it was replaced by a new lifting bridge, some 400 yards down river, which also contained a roadway, and a deviation line was constructed to link with the original route.

The new line was opened to traffic on 21st May 1916, and four signal boxes were involved. At the western end was the Keadby Junction signal box (the original route was to be retained as a freight line to Keadby) with a mechanical frame. Where the new line crossed a canal by a swing bridge was Keadby Canal Junction, sited on the canal bank. A box was erected at the lifting bridge, and where the new and old lines reconnected was Gunhouse Junction.

The area was inadequately served by electric power, and the GCR built its own generator for the scheme. The locking frames for the boxes on the deviation lines were all-electric and supplied by the British Pneumatic Railway Signalling Coy. All passenger lines were fully track circuited, and points and signals electrically motor-operated.

Keadby saw the first installation of three position upper quadrant signals as part of a total scheme, a number of these being installed on the deviation line. These operated semi-automatically, reverting to Danger by the operation of a track circuit in advance of the signal, and were electrically prohibited from displaying the full Clear indication (with the arm vertical) until a full braking distance was available between the next signal at Caution ahead and the Stop signal to which it referred. The three position signals displayed a Caution aspect when the arm was inclined at 45 degrees.

A close up of the arm of the BPRS Coy. three aspect semaphore is shown in **Plate 40**, and one of the signals installed in the scheme appears in **Plate 160**.

Supplementing the new type of signal were conventional lower quadrant GCR signals, examples being depicted in **Plates 169—171**. Ground signals were of the BPRS Coy. standard type as shown in **Plate 117**.

The mechanical locking arrangement for the new swing bridge over the canal at the west end of the deviation line is shown in **Plate 172**. The all-electric locking frames for the Keadby Bridge and Keadby Canal Junction signal boxes, together with two different point mechanisms operated from the latter box are illustrated in **Plates 173—176**.

Plate 171: A Great Central bracket signal at Keadby Canal Junction. The 'doll' is fitted with two subsidiary arms as travel along the former main line via Keadby reduced to yard status with the opening of the lifting bridge deviation line. All arms are motor-operated.

P. Tatlow Collection

Plate 172: A view of the rail approach to Keadby Canal Swing Bridge, showing the mechanical detection locking, used to prove continuity when the bridge was open to rail traffic.

P. Tatlow Collection

117

Plate 173: The electrical locking frame at Keadby Bridge with the B.P.R.S. Co. track diagram, and 'banner' type track circuit indicators. All instruments above the locking frame, including the diagram, were later removed.

P. Tatlow Collection

Plate 174: A single-bladed catch point with adjacent 'switch' notice at Keadby Canal, protecting the Canal Swing Bridge, looking from the Scunthorpe direction. The signal box is in the background to the left of centre.

P. Tatlow Collection

Plate 175: The electrical locking frame at Keadby Canal Junction with the L N E R track diagram visible.

P. Tatlow Collection

Plate 176: A facing point lock and operating mechanism at Keadby Canal Junction.

P. Tatlow Collection

Chapter Six

Signalling Instruments and Accessories

Double Line Instruments

'Space interval' as against 'time interval' working was brought into use in British railways, mainly for tunnel sections, in isolated instances between 1840 and 1850.

Mr. Cooke, a pioneer of electric telegraph for commercial purposes, published a paper in 1842 in which he envisaged a line of railway divided into sections, each of which was governed by its own telegraph and into which no train would be allowed to enter until the previous one had been signalled clear. He argued that if fast express and slow goods trains shared the same metals, when thick fog or wet rails on inclines interposed, maintenance of a safe time interval was hazardous. Given an interval of space instead of time, the incidence of collision would be very much reduced. This was the progenitor of the latter day 'Block System'.

Cooke's system used a deflecting needle indicating either 'Line Clear' or 'Line Blocked' as shown in **Figure 69** the 'normal' position being the former, only being altered for the passage of a train. It was even considered that the indicator was serving as a Distant signal for the station in

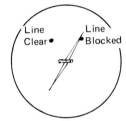

Figure 69: A Cooke dial for the Yarmouth & Norwich Railway (1844).

advance, as the man in rear maintained his signals on the ground to concur with the instrument needle position. Introduced in 1844 over the entire Norwich & Yarmouth Railway, each of the five stations had a complete set of instruments whereby any station on the line could identify the location of any train. It was, however, later abandoned for a less elaborate and costly system.

Most contemporary lines, however, used the single needle 'speaking' type of instrument, which by momentary deflection to one side or the other gave information on the entry or exit of a train. An example of this type is shown in **Figure 70** where one beat to the left indicated 'train in', one beat to the right meaning 'train out'. It was used indiscriminately for both 'up' and 'down' lines, the Sheffield, Ashton-under-Lyne & Manchester Railway using this system through the Woodhead Tunnel from December 1845.

The momentary deflecting needle had one serious drawback. It placed the burden of reliance on the signalman's memory. Even when supplemented by a primitive form of 'train register book', it still did not give the positive indication required for safety. Notwithstanding, the York & North Midland, York & Newcastle and York & Berwick lines proceeded with installations in 1846/7, the Leeds Northern in 1852, and the Newcastle & Carlise in 1852/3.

The next major advance came in a development of Cooke's instrument by Clark of the LNWR. In this, 'Line Clear' was retained, but 'Line Blocked' was replaced by 'Train on Line'. 'Line Blocked' appeared in a different context as a third indication which was in fact the 'normal' position when no current passed. Needle deflection was

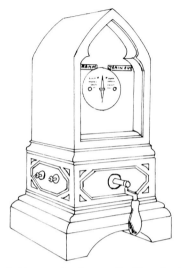

Figure 70: Ashton-under-Lyne & Manchester Railway instrument (1845).

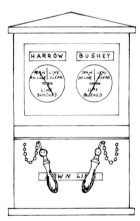

Figure 71: A Clark three position instrument (LNWR) with the 'pegging' of the block.

maintained to either of the two former positions by 'pegging' the control handle, as in the manner of **Figure 71**.

Unfortunately, these early attempts of 'Block' working required railway companies to make expenditure in the erection of 'Block Posts' between stations to avoid delays. In consequence, such 'Block Systems' as were installed were largely for use through tunnels, other places having a combination of 'Block' and 'time interval' systems, yielding a form of 'Permissive Block' operation. The Great Northern in fact reverted to 'time interval' working to speed traffic flow. This later gave way to an inferior system in which the

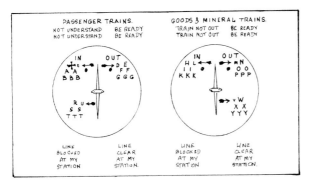

Figure 72: An early Great Northern Railway instrument dial combined with ordinary telegraph. Despite the two dials, one unit controlled only one line.

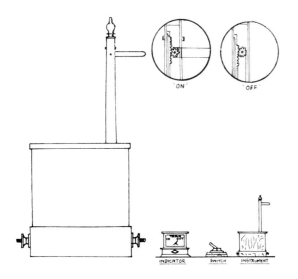

Figure 73: An arrangement of Preece's telegraph used on the Edinburgh & Glasgow Railway.

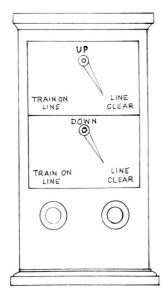

Figure 74: A Tyer's early block instrument of the 1860s, applicable to both 'up' and 'down' lines.

two needles in each direction were used at will for both 'up' and 'down' lines. In the instrument in **Figure 79** the left hand needle referred to passenger trains and the right hand one to engines, goods, cattle and ballast trains. One beat to the left on either needle indicated 'train in', one to the right, 'train out'. The signals 'Line Clear' and 'Line Blocked' were given by momentarily holding both needles over to these words. Advance warnings of train approaches were given to the signalman in advance by pointing the appropriate needle twice to the right. The appliance was also used as a 'speaking instrument' and it is perhaps easy to understand that early signalmen took some time to master the instrument! **(Plate 177)**.

Preece's instrument, used on the Edinburgh & Glasgow Railway is shown in **Figure 73**. A miniature semaphore signal was mounted on top of a box with electrical coils which showed a signalman what the position of his Home signal should have been. When an electro-magnet was energized, it pulled down an armature which was linked to the small signal arm, operating on rack and pinion principle. The apparatus was also fitted with a bell and indicator which showed 'signal on' or 'signal off'.

In the mid-1860s, Edward Tyer developed an instrument which met with Board of Trade approval. The appliance is shown in **Figure 74**, and incorporated constant deflection by using permanent magnets. In use, the signal at one station could only be altered by the signalman in advance. For clarity in definition, a bell was supplied for one line, a gong for the others. A simple bell code was devised for different types of trains, and it is interesting to quote in full:-

Acknowledgement	1 Beat
Passenger Train	2 Beats
Goods Train	3 Beats
Express or Engine	4 Beats
Obstruction on Line	5 Beats
Testing Signal	6 Beats

Two instruments were operated by 'single wire' connections, each being lockfast to avoid unauthorized tampering. Unlike Clark's instrument, if the wire broke, the needle remained unaltered, and was likely to be affected by lightning changing the polarity of the indication.

Notwithstanding, Tyer developed his instrument and the 1879 edition is shown in **Plate 178**. Originally, the normal position was 'Line Clear', but this was later reversed. All Great Eastern double lines were equipped with the instrument by 1884, although the shutter dated from 1882. Many instruments survived into the LNER era.

Instrument operation was as follows. The sending box ('A') sent 'Is Line Clear' on the plunger below the instrument. If so, this was acknowledged by the man in advance ('B') pressing the right hand (white) instrument plunger, thus moving both indicators to 'Line Clear'. When the train passed 'A', he sent 'Train Entering Section' on the bell plunger which was acknowledged by 'B' pressing the left hand (red) instrument plunger, moving both indicators to 'Train on Line'. When 'B' gave 'Train out of Section' on the bell plunger to 'A', there was no needle movement.

Normally, the small (white) screen covered the lower part of the large screen and gave 'Train Passed', both screens covering the 'Line Clear' (white) plunger. Before the

Plate 177: An early 'spelling' type of instrument used at one time on the Great Northern Railway and now in the National Railway Museum at York.

Author

Plate 178: Tyer's Great Eastern Railway double line block instrument, incorporating both 'up' and 'down' line sections within one case.

Author

white plunger could be exposed, both screens had to be swung over to the left to cover the red plunger. 'Train on Line' acknowledgement on the red plunger by 'B' required the large screen to be swung over, thus obscuring the white plunger. The small screen stayed on the left, indicating 'Train on Line'. When 'B' sent 'Train out of Section' the small screen was moved to the right, indicating 'Train Passed'. Both screens were sprung to fly over to left or right as appropriate. When used correctly, this two position instrument was equivalent to a three position type.

A different type of GE two position instrument showed 'Train Arrived' as 'normal' with 'Train on Line' as alternative. Operation was also by white and red plungers but no screens were fitted. If the indicator was at 'Train Arrived' and a train was offered from 'A', 'B' accepted by bell code acknowledgement, but maintained the 'Train Arrived' indication. When 'A' sent 'Train Entering Section', 'B' acknowledged and depressed the red plunger, placing both instruments to 'Train on Line'. When 'B' sent 'Train out of Section', he depressed the white plunger, restoring both instruments to 'Train Arrived', the equivalent of 'Line Blocked' on a three position instrument.

Tyer's three position single wire instruments were also used by the GE. Operated by a momentary current, permanent indications were given. In these units, both 'up' and 'down' line indicators were mounted in the same case, the upper one being worked by the box in advance, the lower one by the box where fitted. The opening above the plunger showed the indication which was manually derived by the signalman rotating the commutator surrounding the plunger, simultaneously depressing the lower left hand button, which action did not affect the needle indication until the plunger was depressed. Installed after 1907, 'Line Clear' and 'Train on Line' required to be given in sequence. If it was required to go direct from 'Line Blocked' to 'Train on Line', as in 'Blocking Back', then 'Line Clear' had momentarily to be given. As in other instruments, plunger operation always rang a bell at the rear box.

Bell signalling on the Great Eastern also included the acknowledgement of 'Is Line Clear' by the special bell code 1-3-3, and not by repetition as on other lines. Bell signals involving indicator movement were always given on white or red plungers, other bell codes being sent on the instrument mounted independent plunger. Indicator movements were therefore always accompanied by a single bell ring.

Although the instruments described above were for double line operation, Tyer's single line block instruments were operated in the same way as the second, having 'Train Arrived' and 'Train on Line' indications, the former being normal.

Three position instruments were normally of the three wire type, one wire connecting the two 'up' line instruments, one, the 'down' line blocks, with the third being used for bells, all between adjacent boxes. Earth formed the return circuit for the three wires, the indicator being held to 'Line Clear' or 'Train on Line' by continuous current, differing in polarity according to indication required **(Plate 179)**.

The instrument was of the single needle telegraph type with a special dial for train signalling purposes. Originally one block unit was supplied for each line in each direction;

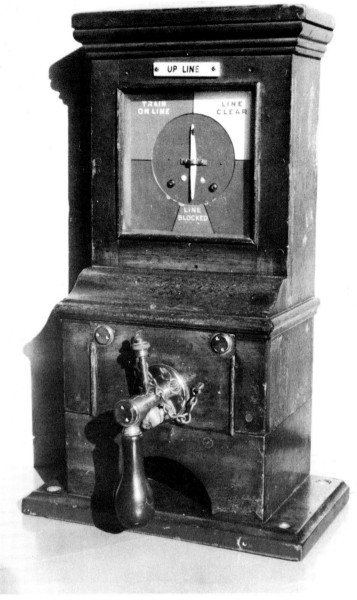

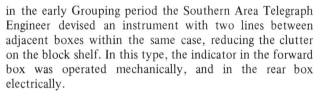

Plate 179: A North British Railway 'pegging' type of instrument. In some receiving instruments the handle was retained for indicating train routing, the designations of the line state being temporarily ignored in favour of 'left' or 'right' temporary positions of the needle. 'Accepting' instruments were equipped with a pin to retain the needle position.

Author

Plate 180: An LNER standard block instrument with a depression key in the lower left to release the instrument to give 'Line Clear'. 'Train on Line' could be given without such additional work.

Author

in the early Grouping period the Southern Area Telegraph Engineer devised an instrument with two lines between adjacent boxes within the same case, reducing the clutter on the block shelf. In this type, the indicator in the forward box was operated mechanically, and in the rear box electrically.

A 'standard' type of block instrument for one line of rails is as shown in **Plate 180**. There were, however, several variations in the handle mechanism, mostly due to former Company practices. The needle adopted the same incline as the handle and current passed only when the handle moved from the vertical. Various devices were used to maintain handle position for contant reading.

On the Great Northern, handle position was maintained by a trigger at the rear of the handle, as in **Plate 181**. The North Eastern and North British used 'pinning', or inserting a pin into the commutator shaft, drilled for both off centre positions. The pin was normally attached to the instrument by a small chain. In LNER periods, the pin was replaced by a form of trigger action bearing on top of the handle, which was sprung loaded, resting in suitable grooves above the commutator. 'Line Clear' was further complicated by the addition of a separate plunger at the lower left of the instrument which, when depressed, activated an electro magnet to lift a metal plate inside the instrument, clearing the commutator for movement. No such action was

Plate 181: A trigger type of handle release fitted to some instruments of similar type to that in **Plate 179** and used on the Great Northern. Unlike the two previous instruments, the operation of 'clearing' the instrument could be undertaken by the use of only one hand. This instrument is now housed in the National Railway Museum at York.

Author

Plate 182 (below): A 'rotary sequence' type of block instrument where the handle moved through 360 degrees. Both instruments are shown; that on the left being at the 'entering' end of the section, the right hand one being in the box at the other end. Note that the cancellation of a 'line clear' indication is by the small plungers at the lower right of each instrument, but the cancellation of a 'train on line' indication can only be undertaken by the sealed release on the right hand equipment. The handle on the 'entering' instrument could be used for route indication purposes.

Author's Collection

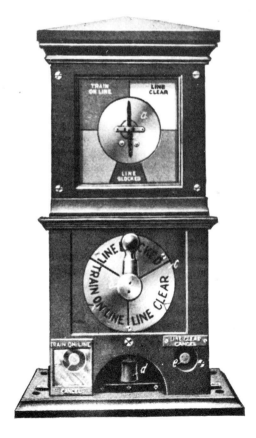

Plate 183: A fine array of LNER type block instruments, but fitted with more modern type commutators for 'accepting', in Brampton Fell box on the North Eastern Railway.

R. Preston

required in passing to 'Train on Line', which could be attained without going through all sequences.

As it was considered that normally the 'accepting' instrument only required handles, instruments in the other signal box were not normally so fitted on the GN and GC, the latter merely mounting the dial on the block shelf. On the NB, two handles were retained, but only one could be 'pinned up', the other serving for routing using the dial in much the same way as the 'speaking telegraph', such action being officially sanctioned.

The Hull & Barnsley used a variation of Sykes 'Lock and Block', but this two wire based system did not long survive Grouping.

The Great North of Scotland originally used Tyer's one wire two position needle block on double line sections, but latterly three position one wire 'Rotary Sequence Blocks' were installed between Aberdeen and Inverurie. The type is illustrated in **Plate 182**.

A fine example of a block shelf for a double line section is given in **Plate 183**, with one type of 'Permissive Block' (where trains could follow each other without the need for 'Train out of Section' being given for the preceding train) in **Plate 184**.

Where provision was not made for bells to be integral with the block instrument, independent single stroke bells were used, examples being in **Plates 185–187**.

Plate 184: 'Permissive block' type of instruments used on the North Eastern Railway. The indicator apertures, at the top of the left hand instrument, show the number of trains in the section, the right hand device giving the bell code for trains coming forward.

R. Preston

'LOCK AND BLOCK' SIGNALLING SYSTEMS

In 1852, Edward Tyer introduced a treadle for electrically indicating the location of trains. In 1869, he patented a device to electrically interlock levers and by using an electrical slot, control the Starting signal of a box from the box in advance. The first complete system of electrical interlocking was patented by Tyer in 1875, and required the concurrence of three separate signal boxes to pass one train through a section. Until then, a signalman could admit a train into an already occupied section merely by clearing his Starting signal. The 1875 patent was developed into a more comprehensive system in 1880 and was adopted, inter alia, by the Hull & Barnsley in 1885, the Great Eastern in 1893 and the North British. A single line control system was introduced on the NB in 1915, making in effect, 'Tokenless Block'.

Sykes system accounted for some 80 per cent of all 'Lock and Block' in Britain, only two others being found on LNER constituents, viz. Blakey & O'Donnell on the GN and Evans on the Great Central.

The principle of 'Lock and Block' was that the signal at one box controlling the entrance to the section ahead could not be cleared until the previous train had passed a Home or Starting signal at the box ahead, a rail mounted electrical contact made, and the latter signal replaced to Danger.

A major disadvantage in 'Lock and Block' was that with the exception of the Evans system, the then widely used 'Section Clear, but Station or Junction Blocked' regulation could not be used. It was also suceptible to human error, although having the capacity to deal with dense traffic flows where many lines were controlled from one signal box.

Plate 188 shows an ordinary Sykes instrument as used on the GER. It dealt with two sections of one line, thus 'up' line sections on each side of a box were controlled by one instrument and the 'down' line sections by another.

The small 'semaphore' fixed on top of the instrument normally stood at 'Clear', rising to 'Danger' when the switch hook was passed over the plunger of the instrument of the advance box or by Starting signal lever replacement if no switch hook was fitted. The arm was, in effect, a two position block indicator of the 'Train Arrived' and 'Train on Line' type, although the precise meaning of the two indications was not always the same in every installation. Three position block indicators sometimes replaced the arm.

The upper slot on the instrument face referred to the Starting signal of a box and showed 'Locked' (normal) and 'Free'. These two indicators were fixed to the upper portion of the lock rod. When the Starting signal lever was 'normal' it was front locked, and when reversed, back

Plate 188: A standard Sykes 'Lock and Block' instrument with semaphore type arm in the upper round case. Although the box referred to was on the LBSCR the same type was used, inter alia, on the GER.

Author's Collection

locked. When the lever was 'normal', 'Locked' was replaced by 'Free' by plunger depression at the box ahead; when reversed, 'Locked' was replaced by 'Free' by the train passing over rail contacts.

The lower slot of the instrument face referred to the section in rear and was normally blank, the alternative being 'Train On' (Train on Line). In some cases, an alternative indication, usually 'Train Accepted' (Line Clear) could be given. With a two position instrument, plunger depression or the upwards movement of the plunger resetting rod brought an indication into view. With three position types, 'Train On' became visible by placing the switch hook over the plunger, although in some installations it came automatically into view by replacement of the rear box Starting signal lever, after the train had activated the appropriate rail contact.

The plunger was used to accept a train. When depressed, 'Train On' (2 position) or 'Train Accepted' came into view and sending a current to the rear box instrument, energized an electro-magnet to negate the pull of a permanent magnet, thus allowing the armature to release the lock rod, which then dropped carrying 'Locked' out of view being replaced by 'Free'. The plunger was locked unless the Home signal lever had been pulled over and replaced, except at a few special locations, and could not be used until the instrument was 'normal'.

The plunger resetting rod dropped when the Starting signal was cleared and it was raised to reset the instrument to normal when the lever was replaced.

The lock rod was raised to show 'Locked' in place of 'Free' by pulling over or replacing the Starting signal lever.

Switch hook operation raised the semaphore arm in the rear box instrument to horizontal and when over the plunger, the latter could not be depressed. The hook was also used when 'Train entering Section' was received from the rear box and also when 'Obstruction Danger' or 'Blocking Back' signals were sent. It was not moved again until clearance bell signals were exchanged. Hook removal was usually accompanied by one beat on the bell to alert the signalman in rear to the lowering of the instrument semaphore.

The switch rod altered the circuit for releasing the Starting signal lock. When raised, the instrument was set to receive current from the box ahead, when lowered, from the rail contact. Rod movement was achieved by pulling over and replacing the Starting signal lever.

Bell signals were exchanged on separate instruments.

The rail contact was fixed to the running rail and although of several different types slight depression of the rail during the passage of a train caused momentary contact to be made, completing a circuit between battery and instrument.

A release key was required for traffic reasons and also to deal with electrical failure. If a previously signalled train was cancelled, insertion of the key release permitted 'Train On' or 'Train Accepted' indications being replaced by a blank at the advance box. If the Starting signal had also been cleared for the train to proceed, 'Locked' was replaced by 'Free' to allow the Starter to be placed to 'normal' in addition to clearing the instrument at the advance box. For this, the key was inserted into a special hole in the instrument shelf. Although the key was necessary to complete a cancellation, it could be used to release a front lock on a Starting signal unless there was an Advanced Starting signal. If train passage over the rail contact failed to release the backlock on the signal, the key was used, but not until 'Train out of Section' bell signals had been exchanged. The key was located on a hook on the instrument shelf.

In some installations, such as the NB, the key was not used, but the instruments were provided with buttons which were operated simultaneously at both ends of the section to obtain a release. An NBR instrument, with outer case removed, is depicted in **Plate 189**.

Blakey & O'Donnell's system instrument differed from a standard three position block in having the words 'Train on Line' replaced by 'Train entering Section'. Two treadles (sometimes combined) were located at the Starting signal of the despatching box one causing the signal to revert to 'Danger', irrespective of lever position, the other placing both instruments automatically to 'Train entering Section' in the absence of the necessary bell signals. If the advance signalman wished to stop a train for which clearance had been given, he merely 'unpegged' his instrument for that section, thus releasing an electrical slot which replaced the signal, also irrespective of lever position in the rear box.

'Line Clear' could not be given for a second train until the first had passed through the section and activated treadles at the advance box which removed the 'Train entering Section' indication.

The only Permissive Lock and Block system was designed by Evans, using a normal three position block instrument altered by the addition of a switch handle between operating handle and instrument dial. Above the dial was a slot through which the words 'ABSOLUTE' or 'PERMISSIVE' were displayed as appropriate. The Starting signal comprised a normal semaphore and a distinctively-shaped small 'subsidiary arm' as in **Figure 75**. While horizontal the subsidiary displayed no light, but when cleared to a vertical position, a small green light was visible. Both arms were worked from the same lever in the box.

When 'Absolute Block' was operative, the instrument switch lay over to the left and 'ABSOLUTE' appeared on the screen, trains being signalled forward as per standard three position block, the main signal arm responding to the lever. When 'Permissive' working was required, the switch was moved to the right, 'PERMISSIVE' appearing on the screen. Simultaneously, an electric motor moved a selector under the floor of the box out of the operating position for the main arm into that for the subsidiary, locking the appropriate Distant signal at Caution.

In practice, Evans' system replaced that whereby a signalman cautioned a train by green flag signals outside the box after stopping and bringing forward. It was the predecessor of the 'Warning' subsidiary signal.

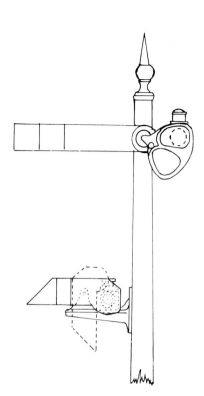

Figure 75: A main Starting signal with a Permissive subsidiary arm bracket mounted below for use with Evans 'Permissive Lock and Block' system. Below, is the type of block instrument that could permit either 'Absolute' or 'Permissive' block working according to the position of the switch above the operating handle. The switch gave a visual indication of the operating method and was also linked electrically to the relevant Distant signal.

Plate 189: The interior of a Sykes 'Lock and Block' instrument as used on the NBR, with a three position dial above and a handle, instead of knob type movement.

Author's Collection

Single Line Systems

The earliest form of single line regulation was by timetable. Trains were timed to cross at specified locations and drivers were issued with 'Starting Orders' which authorized them to proceed thence, where the first arrival awaited the second. With the introduction of the electric telegraph, 'Crossing Orders' were issued to extend the range of the 'Starting Order' if one train was known to be late and the station agents concerned came to a clear understanding that the move would be safe.

Another method of operation used a 'pilotman' who accompanied all movements over the single line unless two or more trains were waiting to proceed in the same direction when he verbally instructed drivers to proceed, (the preceding train, having cleared the section) travelling with the last train. The verbal authority was superseded by the issue of 'tickets'.

Manpower was expensive, and 'pilotmen' were displaced by wooden staffs, endorsed with the section limits and without which no train could enter the single line. Uneven traffic flows also had recourse to the use of 'tickets', drivers taking these from a slot in the end of the staff to ensure sight of the single line authority (**Plate 190**).

Originally 'tickets' were not kept under security, but lockfast boxes were devised for them, the key being the staff, which, when inserted, could not be withdrawn unless the lid was closed. One end of the staff was shaped into one of three configurations viz., round, square or triangular, and no staff could open a box with a different lock shape. An example of the arrangement is shown in **Figure 76 & Plate 191**. Wooden staffs gave way to iron or brass examples of the later type being shown in **Plates 192 & 193**.

Despite 'Staff and Ticket' being safe, (over the first 40 years only four fatal collisions occurred) when the staff was at one end of a section and was required at the other, heavy delays could be incurred in transportation.

Basic signal box equipment at that time involved instruments, staff, tickets and ticket boxes for each direction. In March 1878, Edward Tyer patented an instrument combining all these into one and also eliminated transportation delays in that if no 'Staff Discs', as early 'Tablets' were called, were out, one could be withdrawn at either end although not restorable to the instrument whence it was taken. Special arrangements were required for shunting on to the single line if the train was not to proceed through the section.

The issuing instrument had a cylinder for the 'Staff Discs' at the base of which was a slide with a recess the exact depth and diameter of the Disc. The slide was released electrically from the box in advance, this locking both instruments and precluding further Disc issues. Originally made of metal with a card inset showing the section limits, Discs were later engraved.

The receiving instrument had an upper lid which was raised for the insertion of a Disc and a lower lid inside the machine interlocked in such a manner to catch a Disc passed through the upper lid. When the upper lid was closed

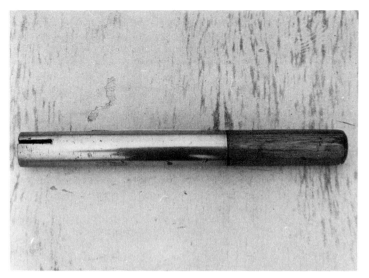

Plate 190: An example of a composite wood/brass train staff fitted with a slot which had an internal spring to hold the ticket. Drivers were required to remove the ticket and take it through the section, after having satisfied themselves that the staff applied to the section concerned. The staff was 16½in. long and 1¾in. diameter, the brass section being $^{3}/_{16}$ in. thick wrapped over the wood core.

Author

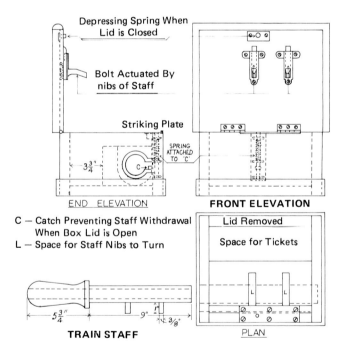

Figure 76: A typical train staff and ticket box. Tickets could only be removed from the box by the presence and action of the staff, although there was nothing to prevent withdrawal of a number of tickets at one time. Tickets could, however, only be presented to a driver in the end of the staff or where no slot was provided, the driver had to see and check the validity of the staff.

Plate 191: A wooden staff and ticket box with a wooden staff, now in the National Railway Museum at York. The brass plates on both items are inscribed with the staff section limits. The keyhole in the box was of a different shape to those for adjoining sections to prevent the use of conflicting staffs.

Author

Plate 192: A solid brass cast train staff, with the end shaped as a key for a ground frame release, as used on the Ballochney Incline, near Glasgow, on the former Monklands Railway section of the North British.

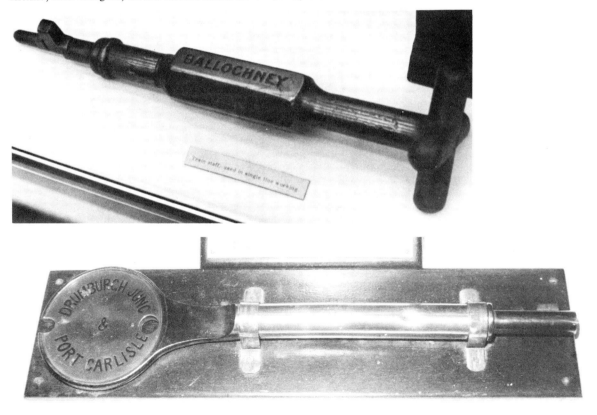

Plate 193: A train staff used by the horse-drawn Port Carlisle 'Dandy' until 1914 and latterly by its steam train successor until 1930/31. The portion of the staff indicating 'section limits' strongly resembled a Tyer's No. 6 tablet (see overleaf), but without the centre hole.

Plate 194: Tyer's No. 6 tablet instrument, showing the side-mounted lever for raising the tablets in the machine to facilitate bottom feed by the slide. The instrument face has been temporarily altered by technical staff in reversing 'up' and 'down' train indications. The machine is shown in the 'normal' or 'both tablets in the machine' condition.

Author

Plate 195: A round brass tablet from a Tyer's No. 6 machine. The centre hole (round, in this example) was of three shapes to prevent contrary insertion in machines. The other two shapes were square and triangular.

Author

after insertion, the lower lid opened and decanted the Disc into a bag in the lower part of the instrument the key of which was held by a lineman who periodically emptied the bag and replaced the Discs in the sending instrument. A counterweight on the lower lid replaced it in position and put the machine in phase with the sending instrument.

The 1878 instrument was, after trials, put into general service in 1880. Each token station was equipped with a sending and receiving instrument for each section, but the two functions were later combined into one machine, linemen only being required to correct token imbalance or remedy machine malfunction. In 1889, the 'cancelling' feature was added, permitting restoration of a tablet taken out in error, which had previously to be taken through the section by foot if there was no suitable train.

The combined instrument was known as 'Tyer's No. 6' and found employment on all the constituent lines of the LNER, many surviving to give service to its successor after 1948. A few were still in service in the late 1970s, although largely superseded by 'Key Token' instruments. An illustration of a 'Tyer's No. 6' is in **Plate 194** and a typical 'tablet' in **Plate 195**.

The method of operation of the 'Tyer's No. 6' was as follows, with 'A' and 'B' representing two token stations. 'A' offers 'B' the train by the appropriate bell signal. If clear, 'B' repeated the code to 'A', holding in his plunger on the last beat to enable 'A' to turn his commutator, causing 'OUT' to appear in his lower indicator and unlock his slide. 'A' then withdrew the slide and removed the tablet. When the galvanometer needle reverted to vertical after 'B' released his plunger, 'A' gave one beat on his plunger causing 'B's' upper instrument to show 'OUT'. When the tablet arrived at 'B', it was inserted into the slide, lettered side downward. 'B' pushed the slide back, raised and lowered the lever, and gave 'Train Out of Section' to 'A', again holding the plunger in on the last beat for 'A' to reverse his commutator. 'A' then pushed his hitherto locked slide back and acknowledged to 'B', pausing slightly on the last beat to allow 'IN' to appear on 'B's' upper indicator. 'B' then gave one beat on the bell to 'A' which restored the latter's lower indicator to 'IN', both instruments being then ready for the next train.

In 'cancelling' a train, 'A' replaced the tablet in his slide, pushed the slide home, reversed his commutator, raised and lowered his lever, and gave the appropriate bell signal to 'B' which was acknowledged and by holding in on the last beat, caused 'IN' to appear on 'A's' lower indicator.

A development of the No. 6 instrument was the 'No. 6 Converted' as in **Figure 77**. It was basically similar to the former except that in issuing a tablet, 'A' required to lift a 'check' on top of the instrument before the slide was free to be withdrawn. On tablet arrival at 'B', the signalman there lifted the cylinder lid for replacement, not in the slide. In cancelling, the tablet was placed in the cylinder, commutator reversed, check lifted and slide pushed home before bell codes were exchanged.

'Tyer's No. 5' instrument was introduced in 1919 on the then single line between Langley and Cuffley on the Great Northern, where it operated as a 'Permissive' tablet machine. The 'No. 5' enabled second and subsequent tablets to be issued before the first had been through the

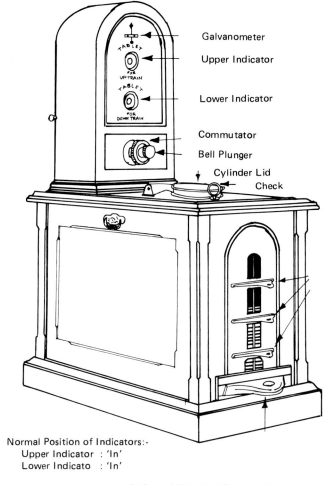

Normal Position of Indicators:-
Upper Indicator : 'In'
Lower Indicato : 'In'

Deflected if the Bell Plunger of a
sending or receiving instrument is depressed

Figure 77: A Tyer's 'converted No. 6' instrument.

the tablet slide was withdrawn enabling its tablet to be restored to the machine or passed through the section. 'Tyer's No. 5' Instrument is shown in **Plate 196**.

Each pair of tablet instruments controlling a single line had generally 24 tablets between them, originally five inches but later altered to four inches diameter. Tablet depth was half an inch, and in addition to being engraved with section name and serial number had a round, square or triangular hole in the centre, no two consecutive sections having the same pattern. Initially of brass, bound with steel edges, aluminium and even fibre was latterly used to reduce costs and weight.

Plate 196: A Tyer's No. 5 'Permissive Block' instrument for single line working. The tablets for this instrument were identical to those for the No. 6 machine.

Author

section. It did not give a positive indication of whether permission had been given or received for tablet withdrawal, but design provision existed to prevent unauthorized tablet issue. Up to 24 tablets were held in a horizontal drum, access being through an aperture on top of the drum casing. Tablets were returned through the same slot. When more than one train required to pass through a section, bell signals were transmitted on the right hand plunger beside the indicator. When permission had been granted from the man in advance to withdraw a tablet, the left hand plungers were operated releasing a catch on the drum, and by turning the commutator, the despatching point magazine was rotated one notch, bringing a tablet into position for withdrawal. The withdrawn tablet was placed in a slide at the base of the instrument, thus freeing from 'Absolute' conditions. This initial tablet was locked in the machine, but subsequent tablets could be similarly withdrawn. When returned to the machine in advance, the drum rotated to its first position and when all had been replaced, the lock on

A number of single lines had sidings or other points too far distant to be operated from the nearest signal box. The shaping of the old train staff acted as a key for local frame release, but obviously the round tablet was not suitable. It was in 1889 that a suitable electrical instrument was devised to overcome this problem and dispense with the old delays incurred with a single staff for each section.

This was the Webb & Thompson Staff Instrument accommodating metal staffs of some twenty two inches in length, subsequent models reducing both sizes of staff and instrument. Usually floor mounted with a long magazine to hold staffs not in use, several different types of operating mechanism heads were used, and for brevity, the NBR system is quoted.

The instrument head was fitted with two dials and a galvanometer **(Plate 197)**. The bell indicator was usually on the right hand side and normally set 'FOR BELL'. After bell code exchanges, the signalman in advance ('B') held down the bell key until the galvanometer needle was vertical, indicating staff withdrawal at the box in rear ('A'). At 'A', the signalman saw the needle deflection caused by 'B', turned the right hand indicator to 'FOR STAFF' withdrew the staff and altered the left hand indicator to 'DOWN (or UP) STAFF OUT' as appropriate. When the staff arrived at 'B', the signalman there deposited it in the pillar, gave 'Train Out of Section' to 'A' and turned the left hand indicator to 'STAFF IN'. 'A' also altered his indicator to concur and both instruments were ready for the next train.

The Webb & Thompson instrument was made by the Railway Signal Company of Fazakerley, and a more compact type was also produced for bench instead of floor mounting, and is illustrated in **Plates 198 & 199**. The working head **(Plate 200)**, was similar although the wording was slightly altered around the left hand indicator. A train staff for the Webb & Thompson instrument is illustrated in **Plate 201**. Operation of the machine was the same as for the larger unit, the example illustrated being employed on the Great Eastern.

Plate 198: A miniature version of the Webb & Thompson instrument, made by the Railway Signal Company of Liverpool. Even the size of the staffs was miniaturized.

Author

Plate 197: A Webb & Thompson staff instrument, showing the top of the staff magazine.

Author

Plate 199 (below): This is a side view, showing staff projections.

Author

134

Plate 200: The head of a miniature Webb & Thompson single line staff instrument.

Author

Plate 201 (above): This is a Webb & Thompson train staff from the Leadburn Junction to Broomlee section of the NBR. It is of solid brass 25¾in. long (including a 'key' portion of 2¾in.) and 1¼in. in diameter. Miniature instrument staffs were shorter and did not have the extreme left hand ring. The provision of a built in 'key' was optional for either type, according to the section for which they were used.

Author

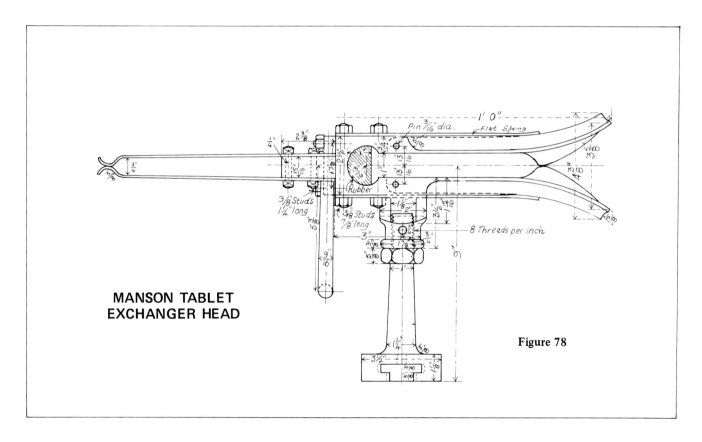

MANSON TABLET EXCHANGER HEAD

Figure 78

Two types of equipment were in use on LNER lines for the exchange of single line tablets at speed.

By the mid-1880s, all tablet exchanges were undertaken by hand and for reasons of staff safety, trains reduced their speeds to about 5 m.p.h. for the operation. Notwithstanding, accidents did occur, and taking the mail bag exchange apparatus as a model, Mr. J. Manson, Locomotive Superintendent of the Great North of Scotland devised a similar scheme for tablets. This was found to be impracticable and was abandoned. Manson is then reputed to have consulted a blacksmith, John Duncan, who had experience in machines for cotton transference in a weaving mill. Duncan obtained permission to examine this plant and having established the principle obtained Manson's approval to erect a standard in Kittybrewster Locomotive Depot for further development. Trials proved a transfer speed of 15 m.p.h. was practicable, and following installation on the Elgin and Grange North Coast line, it was noted that effective exchanges were being made at over 50 m.p.h. Manson did not patent his device and in addition to becoming standard on the GNSR, it was also used on other railways, sometimes in modified form. The North British installed the plant between Hillside and Inverkeillor on the Aberdeen-Edinburgh main line (although restricted to express passenger and fish trains) from November 1911.

The lineside equipment comprised a cast iron pillar with bracket, bolted to a concrete base set into the ground, the bracket supporting a sliding head operated by a lever. The sliding head accommodated a detachable exchanging head, fitted, on the receiving portion, with jaws working against a rubber buffer. Above the receiving head was a delivery spring unit which held the pouch to be picked up by the locomotive. The jaws gripped and withdrew the pouch from the locomotive equipment.

Locomotive equipment was similar to the ground exchanging head, normally lying against cab or tender side, being lowered only to effect the exchange (Plate 202). When diesel multiple units were introduced to the Inverness–Aberdeen line in the mid-1950s, brake compartments were equipped with the exchange apparatus. Lineside equipment was gradually overtaken by an expansion of 'Non Token Block' and phased out, the last examples being on the former Highland Railway near Inverness (Plates 203 & 204).

Tablet pouches consisted of a large reinforced hoop attached to a leather holder in which the signalman placed the tablet. The pouch had a brass-bound ring through which the driver could check the inscription without opening. With the advent of 'Key Tokens', a second pouch was added on the opposite side also with a hole to accommodate inscription reading. Despite the strong construction, pouch lifespan is short, due to impacts at the moment of exchange. Identical pouches are also used for hand exchange, as in Plates 205 & 206.

The other form of apparatus used by the LNER was Whittaker's, (Plate 207), on the Midland & Great Northern Joint from May 1906. The plant was simpler than Manson's and was made at the Melton Constable Works of the M&GN, against a royalty of £1,800. Ground equipment consisted of a metal pillar on which was mounted two separate arms, one with jaws to receive the tablet pouch, the other for delivery having a spring clip. Normally, the equipment lay parallel to the rails, being placed at right angles to it only for exchanges. The upright pillar was fitted with two bevelled wheels with sprocket over a quarter of their face, an integral stop preventing further travel. A balance weight was fitted that was slightly past the perpendicular when correctly set. Exchange impact threw this weight over centre and both arms swung clear of the train, a safety feature not found in GNSR plant. Forty two complete sets, twenty one delivery and twenty one receiving units were provided, generally near signal boxes.

Fitted to most M&GN locomotives was a combined delivery and receiving head. Many engines, including almost all tank types were fitted on both sides to permit tender or bunker first movement. The engine receiver comprised spring jaws with two triggers at the front and a rubber pad at the rear. When out of use, it lay close to the side of the engine, being lowered when exchange was required. Small iron pouches with hoops were used, the top being almost five inches square.

Tablet receiving plant mounted in the '6 foot' is shown in Plates 208 & 209 hand exchange platforms being in Plates 210 & 211.

Plate 202: The Manson type of locomotive equipment fitted to the cab side and shown in the 'normal' position when not required.

Author

Plate 203: The operational head for the ground plant detached from the structure in Plate 204, showing the 'T' section channel by which it was attached. The tablet receiving portion is to the right, with the despatching gear being to the left.

Author

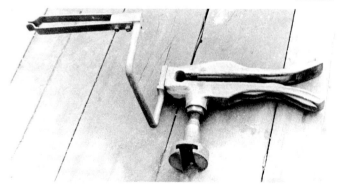

Plate 205 (right):   The pouch for the tablet exchange, showing the positioning of the brass-bound hole for section limit inspection, when used with a Tyer's No. 6 tablet.

Author

Plate 204: A ground-mounted pillar of the Manson type exchange apparatus, located at Millburn Junction box, Inverness. Although of basically identical pattern to the original, as in the case of the equipment in **Plate 203**, minor modifications had been carried out over the years.

Author

Plate 206: The tablet 'pouch' devised latterly for use with the Railway Signal Co. miniature staff.

Author

Plate 207: A Whittaker type of tablet exchange apparatus stand, used on the Midland & Great Northern Joint Line at Gedney, between Spalding and Sutton Bridge.

A. Waterfall

Plate 208: Tablet exchange apparatus at Holbeach West, on the Midland & Great Northern Joint, where siting, in the space between the rails, precluded the use of the type of plant in **Plate 207**.

A. Waterfall

Plate 209: A view of the equipment seen in **Plate 208** showing the position after the exchange had been effected or when not in use. Note the 'hood' over the catching head.

A. Waterfall

Plate 210: A broad type of tablet exchange platform, for hand operations, at Bishop Auckland on the North Eastern Railway. These were of wood construction throughout. The use of two separate platforms was unusual and was resorted to where it was not possible to effect an exchange from the signal box steps. A handrail was provided on three sides of the platform, for safety reasons, although an exchange at speeds greater than that laid down could result in injury by the 'whiplash' of the received tablet.

Author

Plate 211: A narrow tablet platform, from the North British Railway, at Kinniel, on the Bo'ness line. Although of wood construction, the unit rests on old bullhead rail supports, a practice standardized after the Grouping to reduce the hitherto underground timber vertical supports being rotted by dampness or water.

Author

'Non Token Block' was introduced in 1916 on the Lothian lines of the North British near Edinburgh, which were freight only. The instrument face is shown in **Figure 79 and in Plate 212**. When a train was required to pass over the single line, bell signals were exchanged on instrument shelf-mounted tappers, and the receiving signalman ('B') pushed his slide from the 'normal' (mid) position towards the instrument, and pushed in the plunger, locking both slide and plunger. 'TRAIN FROM' appeared in the train indicator panel and his Home signal was unlocked. Needle deflections occurred in both signal box instruments, indicating slide release to the sending box ('A') and when pulled outwards, caused 'TRAIN TO' indication to appear at 'A', releasing the lock on the Starting signal. This signal was restored to 'normal' by a treadle ahead of it. When the controlling lever was subsequently replaced after the arm had been seen to move to Danger it was locked. Even if the lever was not promptly replaced, the signal remained at Danger until the lever was replaced and appropriate clearance obtained from 'B' for the next train. When the train activated a treadle ahead of the Home signal at 'B', it released a 'backlock' at that box and instrument needle deflection indicated that the slide was free. 'B' then replaced the Home signal lever, pulled the slide out to the mid position and depressed the plunger which deflected the needle at 'A'. When 'Train Out of Section' was given, 'A' noting the needle deflection, pushed his slide in the mid position and both instruments were ready with vertical needles for the next train.

A train could only be cancelled if it had not passed the treadle at 'A's' Starting signal. This was done by using normal 'Cancellation' bell signals following which 'B' depressed his 'Acceptance Cancellation' button. 'A' also depressed his 'Sending Cancellation' button which released 'B's' slide and deflected his instrument needle. 'B' then released his cancelling button, placed his slide in mid position and gave one beat on the bell to 'A' who in turn released his cancelling button and acknowledged with one beat. 'B' then depressed his plunger, releasing the slide at 'A' to move to mid position and establish normal acceptance conditions.

At Brunstane Park Junction, three single lines diverged from one, the operation of any three instruments automatically locking the fourth. The track and signalling diagram is shown in **Figure 80**.

In addition to the systems for normal single line operations outlined in this section, some single lines were operated by Tyer's 'two position' block instruments, others by 'pilot guard', which was a variation of 'pilotman' or 'human staff'.

Plate 212: 'Non Token Block' instruments at Niddrie North Junction, Edinburgh, on the Lothian lines. The frame and instruments to the right controlled a portion of the 'Waverley Route', the box controlling trains on two separate levels.

I. Scrimgeour

Figure 79: A front elevation of a Sykes 'Non Token Block' instrument as used on the North British Lothian lines. This system of train regulation continued into the British Railways era outlasting the N B R standard double line block instruments in the same signal box, where these were provided for movements on other lines. The actual operation of the equipment is described in the text.

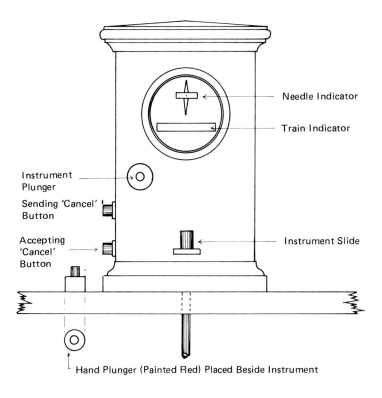

Figure 80: The track diagram for Brunstane Park Junction signal box, showing the position of the track treadles in relation to the signalling. This box operated entirely with the 'Non Token Block' system.

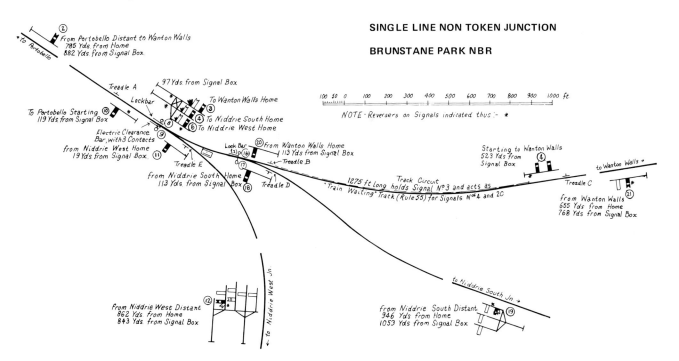

Train Describers — Mechanical

Train route information can be passed from block post to block post or station by numerous means, such as bell code, telephone, telegraph or even block or token instrument, but there are instances where these methods are inconvenient and to meet these circumstances a separate type of instrument developed.

A Tyer's instrument, similar to the example in **Plate 213**, was installed at Newcastle Central about 1900. The appropriate train description was selected and a pin inserted on the dial. A plunger was then pulled and released, causing a drum to rotate inside the instrument until stopped by a catch contacting the pin. When the drum revolved, it set up electrical impulses which were transmitted to the receiving unit generating a similar display. This was acknowledged by the receiving point repeating the display on the top portion of his instrument which was in turn sent to the lower dial on the original transmitting instrument. When the train passed, the pin was withdrawn and the drum rotated to its 'normal' position. Again the operation was repeated in reverse preparing both instruments for the next transmission.

At Edinburgh Waverley (East), a Tyer's type of instrument was modified to operate between the signal box and the station to give platforming details. In this case, repetition was considered unnecessary and the signalman operated both dials. Illustrated in **Figure 81** the top instrument was located in the signal box, the lower one being in the station.

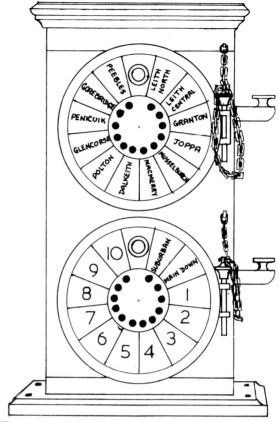

Figure 81: A development of a standard Tyer's type of train describer, of the box to box type, to function between the signal box and a terminal station. This particular North British type operated from Waverley East box, in Edinburgh, to the main station, and gave the originating point of the approaching train and the platform to which it was being signalled.

Plate 213: Tyer's mechanical type of train describer from the Dundee & Arbroath Joint line. This appliance is now in the National Railway Museum at York, as illustrated, but the instrument is not in phase. The dial activating pin is in its holder on the block, the dial giving a positive indication.

Author

Plate 214: The 'Train Ready to Depart' indicator, in Aberdeen North box. The 'flags' moved in response to plunger depression by the platform inspector when a train was clear to move.

Author

Plate 216 (below): A 'Limit of Shunt' indicator. Shunting movement along the main lines, in the opposite direction to normal traffic flow, was limited by a lineside marker which took a variety of forms. A very common feature was direct association with track circuits, the marker being placed on the (wrong direction) approach side of the insulated fishplate. This photograph illustrates an oil lit, 'Limit of Shunt' board, at Bishop Auckland, on the North Eastern Railway, mounted on a plain creosoted wooden post. The marking was a white diagonal cross on a red background, with a clear lamp shining through the central aperture.

Author

Plate 215 (above): A Distant signal repeater for a 'splitting Distant' with provision for all signals 'on', or one signal arm 'off'. The frame locking guarded against erroneous arm display. Similar devices were used as guides for signal wire tensioning. Note the use of the term 'Danger', yet the signals were 'cautionary' only.

Author

Fog Repeating Signals

The duties of fog signalmen were to relay to drivers, by visual and audible means, the position of mechanical signal arms. Where visibility was very poor, or where junction prefocused signals were concerned, balance weight position could be used but on the GE and GN, small repeating miniature signals were provided adjacent to signals and fogging positions a few feet above ground level and linked directly to the signal wire. A Great Eastern arm is shown in **Figure 82**.

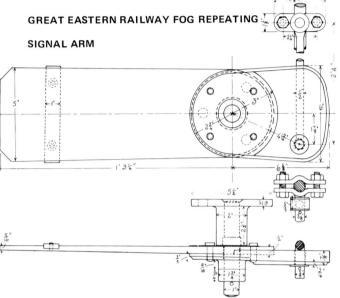

GREAT EASTERN RAILWAY FOG REPEATING SIGNAL ARM

Figure 82: A small arm, used on the Great Eastern Railway, for indicating to fog signalmen the position of the running signal arm. In some instances, the arm was co-acting with the main but in others was independently mounted.

Plate 217: A miniature junction 'fogging' signal, near Doncaster, with 'arms' of upper quadrant type. The signal to which they referred had been removed, hence the absences of wires or rods.

Author

Fog Signalling Indicators

Mechanical signal boxes normally had a defined parameter point which, when visible in conditions of reduced visibility such as fog or falling snow, indicated that there was no need to turn out men for fog signalling duties. This normally took the form of a signal, or lineside structure, but in some instances a specific marker was provided. Illustrating this is the lamp on a short lattice post, used at Hardengreen Junction on the Southern Scottish area, in **Plate 218**.

Plate 218: A 'fogging point' marker light, at Hardengreen Junction, on the former North British Railway 'Waverley Route', near Edinburgh. The lamp is a standard North British oil lit signal type, of a design unique to that railway company.

R. Montgomery

Gate signals were peculiar to the Great Eastern area and were introduced to differentiate between ordinary Distant signals relating to Home signals worked from a signal box and those applicable to level crossing gates where, generally, no Home signal was provided. The special feature was the provision of two lamps, one on each side of the post, both having red or green aspects according to the arm position. This accorded with the pre-1925 requirement of red as the restrictive aspect for Distant signals. The fishtailed arm of the Gate signal was painted red with white lettering.

The last example of a Gate signal on the LNER was removed from Gas House Crossing, Huntingdon, in 1928 and is illustrated in **Plates 219 & 220**. This was mounted on the same post as a Great Northern 'somersault' signal. The signal was on the Great Northern & Great Eastern Joint line, the first signalling being of GN pattern, but maintenance by the GE Engineer, who was also responsible for signalling, led to the addition of the Gate signal arm. The signal was removed to the National Railway Museum at York.

Although most Gate signals were lever-operated, in some instances, such as the Sleaford and Bourne section of the GN, the Gate Distants were worked by having the arm attached to the Gates.

Plate 220: A close up view of the signal arms shown in **Plate 219**, with both arms 'on'. Note the double lamp double aspect of the 'Gate' signal.

P. Tatlow Collection

Plate 221: 'Fireman's Call' plunger boxes were located at certain signals (indicated by a 'D' shaped plate) to obviate the need for a fireman, guard or shunter to proceed to a signal box when the train was detained at the signal. Depression of the plunger caused a 'Train waiting at signal' indication to appear in the signal box and this was acknowledged by the signalman pressing a plunger and thereby ringing a trembler bell in the lineside unit casing. Failure to receive acknowledgement was taken as instrument failure and required the trainman to go on foot to the box. The instrument shown was of Great Northern Railway construction.

Author

Plate 219: A Great Eastern 'Gate' signal below a Great Northern 'somersault' Distant, giving the indication that the gate is closed across the roadway, with the next Stop signal at Danger. A small Great Northern Railway disc shunting signal is in the foreground. The signals were on the former Great Northern & Great Eastern Joint line near Huntingdon.

P. Tatlow Collection

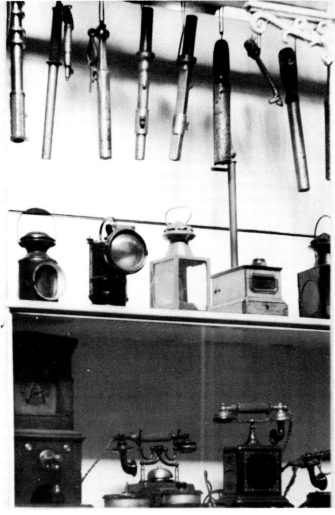

Plate 222: Old signalling equipment, formerly housed in the former LNER Railway Museum at York, featuring (top) a selection of staffs and batons used as signalling authorities or early policemens' batons, (centre) a variety of old handlamps and (bottom) vintage telephones with a 'speaking' telegraph instrument on the left.

Author

Plate 224: A 'Block Switch' enabled signal boxes to be closed for periods by linking electrical services and by-passing the closed box for 'long section working'. This North British example was in Easter Road signal box, Edinburgh. Note the pin on the chain for plunger spring compression. *Author*

Plate 223: Where gas or electricity could not economically be provided, recourse was made to oil lamps for box illumination. This picture shows a self-contained 'Tilley' lamp used in boxes on the North British Railway, this example having been relegated to the locking frame room at Thornton South box, in Fife.

Author

Plate 225: The interior of the 'Block Switch', showing the electrical connecting strips with the pin in position.

LNER

Illustrated in **Plate 226**, is a rare example of a signal that gave permission for movements to take place in apparently conflicting directions simultaneously. In fact the signal was provided more as a point setting guide to drivers when propelling rakes of wagons towards it, the actual movement being under the control of shunters.

Plate 226: A bi-directional common-wired shunting signal, fitted with upper quadrant arms, in the Olympia Cake & Oil Mills yard at Selby, North Eastern Area.

LNER

On the 770 feet long, 152 feet high Staithes Viaduct, on the Yorkshire coast line, between Whitby and Middlesbrough, a wind gauge, or anemometer was installed to give warning to the signalman in Staithes signal box if the wind pressure was too great to permit trains to pass in safety. Installed in 1884, the gauge comprised a circular shield and wind vane. If the pressure of the wind exceeded 28 lbs. per square foot, a bell rang in the signal box which continued to ring until the pressure dropped. During the ringing period, no trains were allowed to proceed on to the viaduct. However, during its existence, the bell rarely sounded, despite the fact that the viaduct was exposed to the full force of gales from the North Sea. The anemometer is illustrated in **Plate 227**.

Plate 227: The wind gauge, on the Staithes Viaduct, in the North Riding of Yorkshire.
Crown Copyright, National Railway Museum

It is only possible to give a very few examples of signalling equipment in these pages, and many must remain 'locked' in the rules and regulations of the various railway companies. Some, such as the North British example of where the door to a signal box could not be locked after the close of duty until a certain lever in the frame had been pulled, thus setting a road into catch points and protecting main line trains, are impossible to illustrate. Many were of purely local significance to meet a specific need, such as the NBR example quoted, and others were strictly parochial to a specific company, often dating back before amalgamations of district lines into the major companies which formed the LNER.

Chapter Seven

Audio-Visual Signals

Audio-Visual Signals

This form of signalling provides an auxiliary aid to train-crew in signal observance and is particularly valuable in reduced visibility conditions, many early devices being patented with this in view. In clear visibility, the equipment also provided a reminder to staff of their location if distracted by locomotive difficulties.

Not all devices were directed at locomotive crews, an 1865 patent (used on the North British) acting on a shoe under the guards van from a ramp placed between running rails **(Figure 83)**.

Basically, track to train signalling took two forms. Firstly, purely mechanical by physical contact between apparatus on locomotive and track, and secondly being by magnetic or electric fields.

A further subdivision can be made into those which gave purely audible indication; audible indication with brake application, and audio-visual types.

Some examples are given below which were used on the LNER constituents.

NORTH BRITISH RAILWAY

ANDERSON'S AUDIBLE SIGNALS —

Figure 83

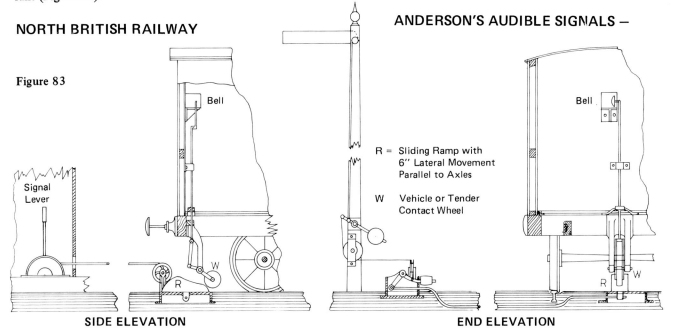

R = Sliding Ramp with 6" Lateral Movement Parallel to Axles

W Vehicle or Tender Contact Wheel

SIDE ELEVATION

END ELEVATION

Boult's System (Magnetic) 1893.

This was experimentally used on Great Northern and Great Central lines, and although effective in operation, even at high speeds, was expensive to install.

Magnets were fixed to the track, being so arranged as to establish a long magnetic field. Locomotives were fitted with an iron armature containing, in a divided gap or space, a small pivoted needle which was deflected by the magnetism collected by the armature.

Permanent magnets were located on the 'approach' side of a Stop signal, which caused the locomotive cab indicator **(Figure 84)** to show Danger. Immediately in advance of the permanent magnets were electro-magnets which, if energized by the signal being Clear, lowered the miniature arm on the locomotive equipment. If a Distant signal only was passed, only the lower miniature arm was activated, if the main signal was clear. The magnets were so arranged that a driver standing at a Stop signal had his locomotive equipment cleared when the signal was cleared. Junction routing was incorporated by using the four left hand circles on the cab indicator. These were termed M2, 1, 2 and 5, 'M2' indicating the main line, with '1' indicating a branch at an ordinary diverging junction. Where there were more than 2 routes possible, '1' and '2' together indicated route 3, 'M2' and 2 giving route 4, etc., the route indicators being energized by a second set of electro-magnets.

Having no physical train to track contacts, the system worked in all weathers.

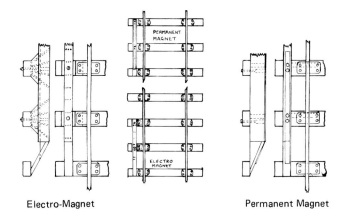

Electro-Magnet

Permanent Magnet

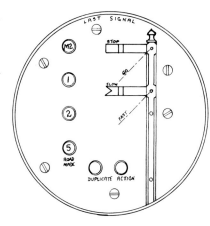

Figure 84: Boult's Cab Signalling. Above are illustrated the locations of the track magnets, assuming a downward travel direction and on the right is the diagram of the indicator provided in the locomotive cab.

Raven's System (Mechanical) 1895.

A purely North Eastern Railway system, it comprised trip levers in the 'four foot' mechanically linked to an adjacent signal, the levers being vertical when the signal was at its most restrictive aspect, thus making contact with locomotive equipment and causing an audible cab indication and partial brake application, the latter being reset by the driver. A Clear signal lowered the levers and no contact was made. The apparatus did not differentiate between Home and Distant signals on the same post. Track equipment is illustrated in **Plate 228**

Although a large proportion of the North Eastern Railway was covered by the system, a basic disadvantage was the mechanical contact, and as line speeds increased, strain was apparent on both locomotive and track fitments, rendering either or both liable to damage.

LNER standard Pacific locomotives allocated to the North Eastern area were fitted with the apparatus and those which were liable to work over the Forth Bridge were fitted with a device that lifted the locomotive equipment clear of the trough-type girders.

The system lasted in use until October 1933 when it was abandoned.

Plate 229: The type of contact shoe fitted to North Eastern locomotives for the Raven AWS system. This particular example was fitted centrally for experimental purposes.

Plate 228: Track equipment linked to the signal for the Raven fog signalling system, with the contact plates in the raised position.

Crown Copyright, National Railway Museum

MILLER'S SYSTEM
LOCOMOTIVE EQUIPMENT

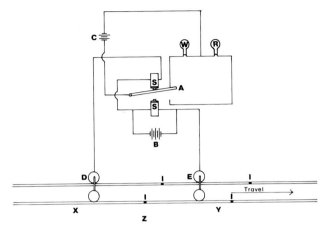

A   Armature pivoted at left.
B   Battery for solenoids.
C   "   "   bulb illumination.
D   Locomotive wheels.
E   "   "   .
I   Insulated rail joints (staggered).
R   Red bulb.
S   Solenoids.
W   White bulb.
X,Y Track Circuit Feeds
Z   "   "   Battery

Figure 85

Figure 86

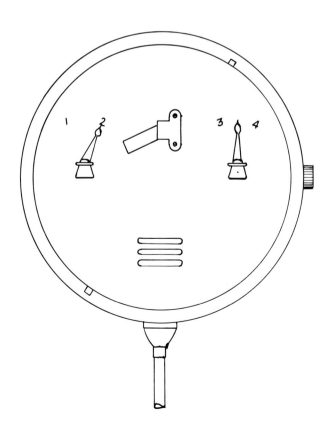

Miller's System (Electrical) 1903.

This required the use of track circuits for operation, together with a small dynamo on the engine. Electrical signals of red and white lamps were cab-mounted, being energized by electro-magnets according to the state of the track circuit **(Figure 85)**.

A trial installation was made between Crowden and Woodhead, on the Great Central, in February 1903, although it gave no guarantee that any obstruction on the line was adequately protected. The results were moderately successful, but failure to counter severe Pennine weather conditions mitigated against full scale development. An additional feature was the requirement for certain parts of the locomotive to be insulated. A second experiment was proposed through Woodhead Tunnel on the 'up' line, but as this was to have been only for freight trains, retaining Absolute Block for passenger trains, it was not carried out.

Although visual indications were given to drivers, there was no connection with train brakes and did not fully give the sought after independent control.

Figure 85: This outlines the locomotive circuit. The direction of the current between Y and X determines whether A is attracted up or down to light the red or white lamp. When the current flows from X to Y, then A is attracted downward, lighting the red lamp and indicating tracks ahead are occupied. When 'Clear', the current passes from Y to X via E to D, so that A moves upwards and the white lamp illuminates. The battery B provides a local circuit through the lower solenoid S and also holds A against either S when passing through the block. When an insulated joint is reached, circuit B through upper solenoid S, by way of the rail back to E, is broken and with the lower S still being energized, A falls and illuminates the red lamp. Thus every time a locomotive passes an insulated joint, it receives a red cab signal, unless the 'Clear' impulse from the track relay operates to keep the white lamp alight.

Raven's System (Electro Mechanical) 1905.

In this, a ramp was placed in the 'four foot' at a Distant signal, supplemented by a ramp outside each running rail. Further electrically-linked ramps were laid in the 'four foot' between Distant and Home signals. A rotary switch on the engine made contact with the outside ramps and a steel 'shoe' contacted these in the rails. A bell was provided in the cab, together with a visual indicator **(Figure 86)** giving junction route settings. If the Distant was Clear, an engine passing over the ramps completed a circuit causing a bell to ring in the cab and also giving a visual Clear signal. If the signal was at Caution, the bell still rang, but the visual indicator gave a Danger position. If the signal was cleared after the engine had passed, the intermediate ramps altered the visual indicator.

The system could not adequately be worked where third or fourth rail electrification was present. It was installed for a few miles near Newcastle upon Tyne in 1907, with an improved version on the Richmond branch in 1910, but it was not developed.

Figure 86: The indication given to a driver by the display shown here is that the line is clear to diverge on to a branch away from the main line. No Distant signal indication was given.

Sykes-Tiddeman System (Electro-Mechanical) 1921

Originally devised by E. S. Tiddeman, Chief Locomotive Draughtsman of the GER, in 1912, experiments took place on the Seven Sisters, Loughton and Epping branches of the GER before the final system was installed in 1921 at the Seven Sisters end of the Palace Gates branch.

A fixed ramp was employed, insulated and placed in the 'four foot' a short distance before reaching the Distant signal, and immediately after passing the Home or Stop signal. When the signals were Clear, the ramps were electrically-energized, otherwise they were dead. The ramp for the Distant signal gave a lift of 1½ inches to the locomotive contact shoe, the Stop signal ramp giving a lift of 2½ inches.

The locomotive apparatus (Figures 87 & 88) comprised a spring-loaded plunger with an insulated shoe mounted on the locomotive framing by a bracket. The plunger also carried a hinged lever or trigger which, in normal position, held the air valve closed. When the main plunger came into contact with a track ramp, the hinged lever cleared the air valve lever and if not electrically-restrained, allowed the air valve to open and released the air in the train pipe to escape, applying the brakes to the train, at the same time giving audible warning to the driver by sounding a whistle.

The driver could reset the gear by pressing the push valve in his cab which admitted air from the main reservoir to enter the cylinder mounted on the main bracket. This, via the bell crank and slotted link, pushed the toggle links into the straight position, enabling the hinged lever to drop back into position against the projection of the air valve lever and reset the valve. A safety arrangement in exhaust ports prevented leakage of air through the cab push valve resetting the equipment.

If the signal was Clear, and the ramp electrically-energized, the insulated shoe picked up the current and transmitted it to the electro-magnet which held the toggle links in position and therefore the air valve closed. A wire from the circuit could also be used to ring a bell in the cab and give a positive indication of the Clear signal.

In the case of the higher Stop signal ramp, the extra one inch lift to the plunger enabled a spring-loaded bolt to engage with a slotted hole in the main plunger, which was thereby held in the raised position and could only be reset from ground level by the driver. The bolt was located at the rear of the bracket, as was the resetting plunger.

When the Stop signal was Clear, the bolt was prevented from engaging in the main plunger slot as long as the toggle links were held straight by the magnet.

The audible warning, given by the Distant signal being 'on' was not as intense as when the Stop signal sounded, and in the latter case, a full brake application was made immediately.

When passing over ramps in the reverse direction, a reverse current was used at the ramps which energized the electro-magnet but as the wire to the bell was taken through a polarity switch, the reverse current was earthed and the bell prevented from ringing.

Although efficient in operation, giving a warning at the Distant signal and an absolute stop at the Home, both with audible warnings, the system was confined to the one branch, and after 1923 further expansion was curtailed. The system was designed to work with Sykes 'Lock and Block' signalling.

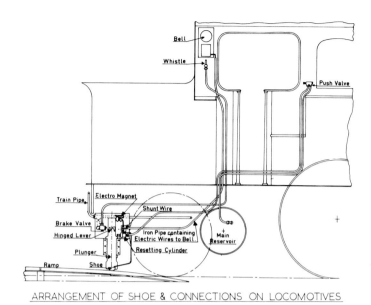

ARRANGEMENT OF SHOE & CONNECTIONS ON LOCOMOTIVES

Figure 87 (above): This shows the general arrangement of the locomotive equipment relative to the track ramps.

Figure 88 (below): An enlargement of the connections on the locomotive 'shoe' bracket.

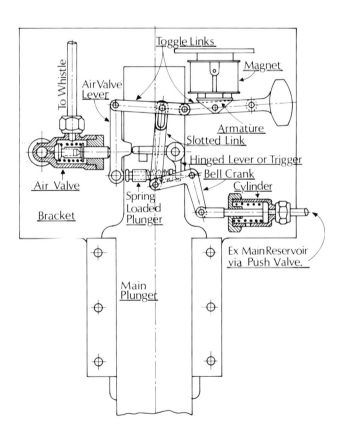

Reliostop System (Mechanical) 1916

This was installed by the Great Central Railway on 11 track miles (5 route miles) at the London end of their line. It was extended until by 1923 some 40 route miles were equipped.

Track equipment was placed adjacent to, but outside, the running rails. Firstly, a simple contact mechanism was placed 200 yards before reaching Distant signals which gave a constant audible warning and brake application which a driver could reset. A second type was similar but operated in conjunction with the signal wires, another variation, also signal wire operated, being sited at Home signals. Trackside plant is illustrated in **Plates 230–231**.

Locomotive apparatus, illustrated in **Plate 232**, comprised contact equipment linked to the train brake pipe and gave an audible indication when a signal that had not been cleared was passed. At Distants, this could be reset from the cab, but at Stop signals, resetting could only be peformed from the trackside.

Lineside plant had a spring fitting incorporated to permit 'wrong direction' working without equipment activation.

Development was suspended after the formation of the London & North Eastern Railway and although the existing plant continued for a short time, it was subsequently removed.

Plate 230: An end elevation of a 'Reliostop' track-side unit.

P. Tatlow Collection

Plate 232: A tender-mounted example of locomotive equipment, of the 'Reliostop' system, on a Great Central locomotive.

P. Tatlow Collection

Plate 231: A side elevation of the trackside-mounted 'Reliostop' unit.

P. Tatlow Collection

Chapter Eight

The Signal Box

The Signal Box

Brief mention has already been made about the evolution of the signal box from the simple hut provided for the protection of the 'policeman' against inclement weather.

Although the claim for the first British signal box was made for Cowlairs, on the Edinburgh & Glasgow Railway, this is open to question, by definition **(Plate 233)**. Certainly, as more complex signalling requirements developed, more adequate buildings were provided and each of the LNER constituent lines adopted a certain degree of uniform styles, if not for the complete line, then for specific sections of it. In addition, signalling contractors normally included signal box designs in their own catalogues, and occasionally these were used, normally 'customised' to railway specifications.

Signal boxes were sited, wherever possible, to give the best view of lines under their control, bearing in mind the then current mechanical limitations imposed by point rodding, a factor that resulted in boxes being built in certain location within close proximity of each other. On the GN approaches to London, separate boxes were built to control 'up' and 'down' lines.

Building materials were usually timber, brick and stone, the proportions in many cases being determined by local soil conditions and availability of materials. Roofing materials were normally tiles, with zinc or similar materials for gutters, rainstrips etc. Occasionally, embellishments in the form of finials or decorative bareboards were added. The main structure in earlier boxes tended to be of stone or brick with sash windows, but latterly wooden upper structures on stone or brick bases predominated. In this form windows which opened were of the sliding type. The length of the box was determined by the overall length of the lever frame with additional space at each end and in some larger boxes the frame was divided in the centre to permit the signalmen access to the front of the box (he normally faced the traffic) for verbal communication with train crews. Windows were normally placed at the front and round the sides as far as level with the rear of the locking frame, doors also being fitted with glazed panels as required. Windows were also placed in the rear of the box when traffic requirements dictated.

The height of the operation floor was normally between 8 feet and 10 feet above rail level, the lower level of the windows being about 3 feet to 4 feet higher. Where clarity of vision was required over intervening road bridges, sidings, etc., the operating floor was pitched higher. Where space for a lineside structure was restricted, the operating floor could project out of the track, or in some cases the entire signal box was built on a metal gantry over the tracks, but operationally the disadvantage was that it impaired ready conversation with traincrews.

Most boxes were fitted with outside balconies which permitted outside window cleaning and also acted as repositories for paraffin handlamps for handsignalling purposes which were continuously lit after dark for Rules purposes, such signals, being given outside the box, being hand held.

Doors to the box normally opened on to a landing, the steps up to this landing being so arranged to give a man descending them a good view of approaching trains. Where the steps finished at right angles to the track, a safety barrier was often provided.

The nameboard was normally of wood with separate cast letters screwed to it within a decorative wooden frame, but some had vitreous-enamelled plates **(Plates 234–237)**.

Lavatory accommodation varied according to local conditions. Some were fitted as part of the box structure with direct access from operating floor, other locations being on the landing outside the operating room, on ground level under the box or the stairs, or even in a separate structure within earshot of the block bells. In some cases where a box was built on a station platform, the station facilities served.

On the operating floor was located the lever frame, surmounted by a board which gave the description of points or signals operated, the locking being indicated on each individual lever, either by paint or separate plate. Lever tops were normally of polished steel, lovingly tended by the signalmen, electrical control levers having shortened lever tops to mechanical control levers. Over the frame was the block shelf, upon which rested non token instruments, signal repeaters, track circuit indicators, block switches, point indicators etc. With the advent of electric locking, this fitment over the levers took the form of an illuminated diagram.

In mechanical boxes, the block shelf was surmounted by a layout diagram showing the position of all signals, points, etc., controlled. This was normally in a glazed frame suspended from the roof. A gradient profile of the section(s) of line on either side of the box was usually nearby. A typical diagram is shown in **Plate 238**.

Train movements were recorded in the train register book which reposed on a sloping top desk, usually with cupboards underneath, on the opposite side of the box from the lever frame. An accurate mechanical clock, regulated daily, was within easy sight of the signalman and lockers were supplied for each person in the box.

Heating was provided by coal fires or other appliances, not only for the benefit of providing heating and cooking facilities, but also to prevent dampness as this was liable to affect the efficient working of electrical equipment and also to cause rusting in the interlocking apparatus.

Lighting was dictated by local circumstances, being either oil, gas or electric. Oil and gas generally had great longevity, often being retained when nearby buildings had been supplied with electricity.

Underneath the operating floor level was interlocking equipment which took up most of the available space. Signal and point connections passed out of the box through an aperture just above ground level, the openings being framed by old rails, wood, stone or concrete blocks, or metal beams. The direction of rodding or signal wires was usually altered outside the aperture by wheels, cranks, etc., bolted to a wood beam inset in the ground.

In the lower section of the box, windows were usually provided initially for the assistance of signal fitters and others whose duties involved locking checks, but these frequently became neglected or broken losing their practical use and were subsequently bricked up or infilled. In most boxes, a rather crude workshop type of facility existed for the use of Signal & Telegraph Department staff.

One of the most difficult aspects of the study of signal boxes is the determination of a Company style from pre-1923 practice and drawings of signal boxes **(Appendix One)** merely illustrate basic types from most major LNER constituents.

Various dimensions of interior fittings of signal boxes relative to the rail level and block instrument shelf are shown in a table at the end of this section.

Mechanical frames used in signal boxes varied with by far the largest element coming from signalling contractors, many of whose frames were embossed with the purchasing line's initials, although some companies such as the North Eastern, developed its own pattern which was made in its own workshops.

The comparative autonomy of the area engineers after 1923 led to the continuation of former Company styles until the 1940s when economy and austerity predominated. Company styles are illustrated in **Plates 239–365**.

Plate 233: Claimed, erroneously, to be the oldest signal box in the world, that at Cowlairs, Glasgow is certainly a strong contender for the London North Eastern laurels. Dating from 1842, it survived until 1911.

LNER

Plate 234: Plain lettering screwed to an unadorned board, used at Arisaig, the most westerly signal box on the British mainland.

Author

Plate 235: A decorative wood frame was given to Great Central boxes, the lettering used also being somewhat 'heavier set' than was customary. Note the contraction of the word 'EAST'.

Author

Plate 236: Vitreous enamel nameboards were common on the North Eastern, where the main colour was brown with cream lettering and edging. Eskdale Mines box was located between Sleights and Grosmont.

Author

Plate 237: The North British also favoured vitreous enamelled nameplates and two basic colour schemes predominated, these being white letters on a blue back (usually without borders) and blue on a white back. One of the latter is still in use at Corrour on the West Highland line.

Author

Plate 238: Signals at Bellingham Station were operated by porter signalmen, and for their guidance the standard type of signalling diagram was enhanced by a lever-pulling guide.

Author

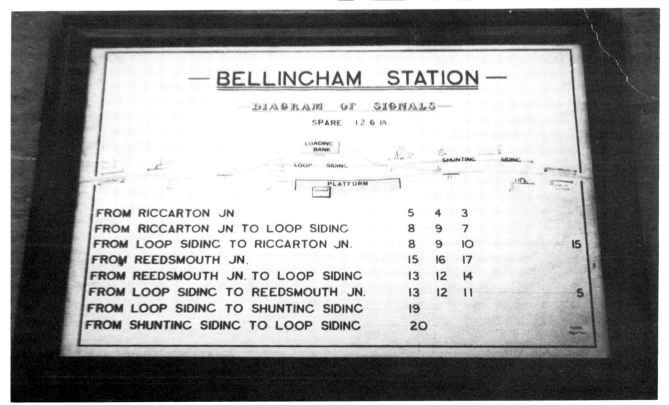

— BELLINGHAM STATION —

DIAGRAM OF SIGNALS

SPARE 12 6 18

FROM RICCARTON JN.	5	4	3	
FROM RICCARTON JN. TO LOOP SIDING	8	9	7	
FROM LOOP SIDING TO RICCARTON JN.	8	9	10	15
FROM REEDSMOUTH JN.	15	16	17	
FROM REEDSMOUTH JN. TO LOOP SIDING	13	12	14	
FROM LOOP SIDING TO REEDSMOUTH JN.	13	12	11	5
FROM LOOP SIDING TO SHUNTING SIDING	19			
FROM SHUNTING SIDING TO LOOP SIDING	20			

Plate 239: A Manchester, Sheffield & Lincolnshire Railway (later Great Central) wooden vertical board built signal box, at Meadow Hall, north of Sheffield.

N. D. Mundy

Plate 240: Marshgate Goods box, Doncaster, of similar type but with a reduced glazing area. Note the use of the double boards for the name.

Author

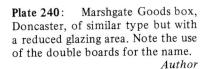

Plate 241: A hipped roof type of vertical board box, with increased glazing area, at Ecclesfield, on the Midland & Great Central Joint.

N. D. Mundy

Plate 242: Wellowgate signal box, Grimsby, of the vertical board type but with gable ends and supplementary glazing for level crossing supervision.

Author

Plate 243: A Great Central style wooden signal box, located on the station platform of New Holland Pier which projected over the River Humber.

Author

Plate 244: The station platform surrounds the base of the brick built signal box at the easterly divergence of the Great Central Railway's Barnetby to New Holland and Grimsby lines. The modern nameboard, which replaced the original, gives the location as Brocklesby. Note the wooden construction at the end, above the window level.

N. D. Mundy

Plate 245: The trim wooden signal box, at Brancliffe East Junction, near, Shireoaks, on the Great Central Railway.

N. D. Mundy

Plate 246: Bentley Junction, near Doncaster, but on the Great Central Railway, is the location for this all wood signal box, which features a landing at the top of the access steps.

Author

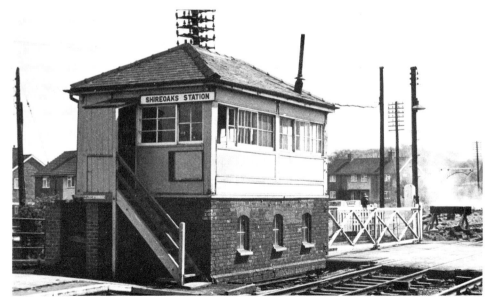

Plate 247: Shireoaks Station was on the Great Central Railway between Sheffield and Worksop. The signal box features narrow vertical boarding on the exterior above the brick built base. Three windows are inset into the base for lighting the locking, and the roof is of the 'hipped' type.

N. D. Mundy

Plate 248: Fretted eaves boards adorn the end of this wooden Great Central signal box at Warsop Junction on the Chesterfield and Lincoln line. Some evidence of ground subsidence is visible in this colliery area.

N. D. Mundy

Plate 249: The fanlight over the end windows, in the signal box at Tuxford Central, has been blocked in. The surrounding woodwork is laid in a vertical direction and no protection is provided over the entrance doorway against the prevailing winds.

N. D. Mundy

Plate 250: Access from the ground is direct into Skellingthorpe signal box, on the Lancashire, Derbyshire & East Coast Railway, (later GCR), west of Lincoln. The adjacent level crossing gates are of wood with metal bars but, unlike that at Shireoaks, a vertical wooden inset is made between each cross piece. The gates are set at an angle to the running rails, the red 'targets' being set centrally over rail centres.

N. D. Mundy

Plate 251: The Lancashire, Derbyshire & East Coast Railway, (later GCR) wooden box at Chesterfield Market Place.

C. T. Goode

Plate 252: Roxton Sidings box, between Brocklesby and Grimsby, of Great Central type with a 'somersault' signal adjacent.

N. D. Mundy

Plate 253: A later type of Great Central 'standard' box, at New Basford, between Nottingham and Chesterfield.

C. T. Goode

Plate 254: One of the largest GCR signal boxes is that at Wrawby Junction, near Barnetby, where the main line from Grimsby divided into three main routes, these being to Doncaster, Gainsborough and Lincoln.

Author

Plate 255: Evening sunshine highlights the level crossing gates at Habrough, the point of divergence of the GCR lines from Grimsby to New Holland and Barnetby and to Wrawby Junction.

Author

Plate 256: Harbour Junction signal box, King's Lynn, is an example of Great Eastern wood construction, although the steps are of a modern type, as is the landing. The box was located on a spur from the main Ely to King's Lynn line to the M&GN Joint line at South Lynn.

N. D. Mundy

Plate 257: Orwell signal box, situated between Ipswich and Felixstowe is fitted with decorative barge boards beneath the eaves round the signal box. Note the planking over signal and point rigging at the base of the cabin.

N. D. Mundy

Plate 258: Decorative eaves boards, unusual window framing and verticals on the wooden horizontal boarding are features of the GER box at Brundall, six miles from Norwich on the Yarmouth line.

N. D. Mundy

Plate 259: A wooden 'platform' type signal box mounted on a metal gantry, at Stratford Southern, on the Great Eastern Railway, on the low level lines.

Author

Plate 260: Ground space restrictions led to the adoption of this unusual design of wooden signal box, at Stepney East, on the Great Eastern Railway, on the Fenchurch Street to Stratford line.

N. D. Mundy

Plate 261:   The unusual box at Trumpington, one mile south of Cambridge on the 'down' GER line, between the junctions to the LNWR to Bletchley, and the GNR to Hitchin. In this box, the width exceeded the length.

N. D. Mundy

Plate 262:   Timbered from operating floor level to eaves was the Saxby & Farmer built signal box at Custom House, on the North Woolwich line.

Author

Plate 263: Wooden construction above the operating floor, at Gunton signal box, between North Walsham and Cromer, on the Great Eastern line. Note the boarding across the lines and the receiving post to facilitate tablet changing.

N. D. Mundy

Plate 264: Chelmsford box was sited over the station buildings, a verandah being provided over the canopy for train sighting purposes.

Author

Plate 265: The branch line terminus and signalling at Buntingford, on the Great Eastern Railway, with a small glazed projection from the box to aid visibility past the water tower.

H. C. Casserley

Plate 266: Ipswich Station box, of predominantly wooden construction, on the station platform. Note the decorative wood below the cabin windows, which are of an unusual pattern.

Author

Plate 267: The decorative, but disused, signal box of brick and timber type, at Cambridge Mill Road, with a reduced height window and an observation 'lookout' at the far end adjacent to the road bridge.

Author

Plate 268: The high roof and decorative ridge tiling, on the predominantly brick platform-mounted signal box, at Wivenhoe, on the Great Eastern Railway. This location, also spelt Wyvenhoe, was the junction station for the Brightlingsea branch on the Colchester to Clacton line.

N. D. Mundy

Plate 269: A substantial amount of this platform-mounted box, at Elsenham, on the Great Eastern Railway, is built of brick. Elsenham was 5½ miles north of Bishop's Stortford, on the London to Cambridge line, and was the junction for the Thaxted branch.

N. D. Mundy

Plate 270: Panelled eaves boards, distinctive glazing, valancing and barge boards were incorporated in Bealings signal box, between Ipswich and Wickham Market, 76 miles from London.

N. D. Mundy

Plate 271: Another platform-mounted, basically brick, box at Attleborough, on the Great Eastern Railway's Norwich to Thetford lines. The end steps are not original.

N. D. Mundy

Plate 272: The brick structure at Brandon, 16 miles from Ely on the cross-country GER line to Thetford and Norwich.

N. D. Mundy

Plate 273: North Walsham is a standard wooden Great Eastern Railway box, platform-mounted and fitted with a 'lookout' for increased visibility. It was located on the 'down' side of the line between Norwich and Cromer.

N. D. Mundy

Plate 274: The high roof brick box at the GER terminus of Southminster on the branch from Wickham on the Shenfield to Clacton line. Although the locking frame windows have been bricked in, the box still retains the very full railings along the front of the main operating floor glazing. Note also the cross track boarding to facilitate hand tablet exchange.

Author

Plate 275: Donington Road was another typically Great Eastern pattern box, on the Great Northern & Great Eastern Joint line, between Spalding and Sleaford, of all wood construction but with fully glazed ends.

N. D. Mundy

Plate 276: Saxilby box, between Lincoln and Gainsborough, was a brick and timber version of the type shown in **Plate 252**, but with the stove located at the front of the box resulting in the 'blanked off' portion in the centre of the front glazing. Note the suspension and length of the crossing gates, each spanning both sets of metals.

N. D. Mundy

Plate 277: The Great Northern Railway pattern all wood signal box, at Misterton, on the Great Northern & Great Eastern Joint line.

N. D. Mundy

Plate 278: Martin Road level crossing box, on the Great Northern & Great Eastern Joint line is, of basically, a Great Eastern wooden construction pattern, although equipped with a modern chemical toilet in place of the original.

N. D. Mundy

Plate 279: Sykes Junction box, of GER pattern, was 1½ miles south of Saxilby and marked the junction between the main Great Northern & Great Eastern Joint line and the 3 mile Torksey line. It is of all wood construction, albeit without railings on the verandah along the front.

N. D. Mundy

Plate 280: The all wood Great Eastern pattern box, at Blotoft, on the Great Northern & Great Eastern Joint line, between Spalding and Sleaford. Note the virtual absence of eaves overhang. The box controlled access to a private siding between Donington Road and Helpringham stations. Despite the appearance of the nameboard, the name was all one word.

N. D. Mundy

Plate 281: A predominantly brick equivalent of the box in **Plate 277**, at Haxey, on the Great Northern & Great Eastern Joint line between Gainsborough and Doncaster. The station name was Haxey & Epworth.

N. D. Mundy

Plate 282: The Great Northern & Great Eastern Joint Keveston Siding signal box, at Saxilby, was of all wood construction. The level crossing gates were suspended from cast uprights, the details of the hanging spars being well defined.

N. D. Mundy

Plate 283: The small timber signal box, at Kirkby Laythorpe, between Sleaford and Boston, on the Great Northern Railway. Note the repositioning of the level crossing gate to the far side of the box and the consequent infilling of the track with timbers.

N. D. Mundy

Plate 284: Stafford (Venables) signal box, on the GNR Stafford and Uttoxeter line, of timber construction, with a large glazed area to the glazing at the side. Note the provision of locking frame windows and the signal finials used for decoration on the roof.

N. D. Mundy

Plate 285: The large wooden signal box, at Loversall Carr, on the Great Northern Railway, with plain horizontal boards without locking frame windows. The box was situated 3½ miles south of Doncaster on the East Coast Main Line.

N. D. Mundy

Plate 286: The small vertical board construction wooden signal box, at Botany Bay, on the Great Northern Railway, 2½ miles north of Retford, on the East Coast Main Line. Both level crossing gates are on the same side of the road crossing. Locking frame windows are in the end of the box.

N. D. Mundy

Plate 287: A brick and timber box at Doncaster, identified by the single word 'Carr'. Note the absence of locking frame windows and the 'double finial' on the barge boards at the end. The box was responsible for signalling goods and engine lines only and did not participate in main line work.

Author

Plate 288: Doncaster 'C' box is of all wood construction, but with an overhanging operating floor level. It did not participate in main line workings.

Author

Plate 289: Arksey signal box, on the Great Northern main line, is of brick and timber construction with a single locking frame window. Arksey Station was joint between the GNR and the Lancashire & Yorkshire Railway, the latter working over Great Northern metals from Askern Junction through to Doncaster.

N. D. Mundy

Plate 290: The brick and timber box, at Bawtry, almost midway between Retford and Doncaster, on the GNR portion of the East Coast Main Line. This box has horizontal boarding and a toilet on the landing. In addition to main line work, the box controlled access to two passenger loop lines and a refuge siding.

N. D. Mundy

Plate 291: A long brick and timber box, without locking frame windows, at Spalding No. 2, on the Great Northern Railway. Note the brick extension at the right hand end with the glazed door for entry to the locking. Spalding Station was joint with the GNR, GER and M&GN companies, the last two running into it over GN metals.

N. D. Mundy

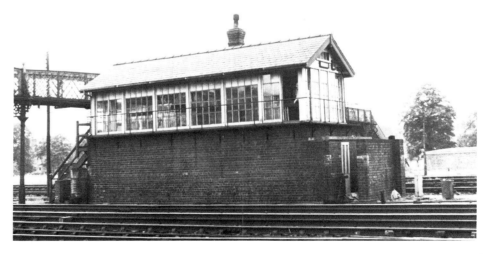

Plate 292: Kimberley signal box was unusually sited on the platform ramp and was fitted with an unusual style of barge board. Note the platform exit gate at the top of the ramp and the timbered level crossing surface. The crossing gates still permitted access between platforms when closed to rail traffic. Kimberley was situated between Nottingham and Derby on the Great Northern.

N. D. Mundy

Plate 293: Bentley Colliery box, on the Great Northern and the Hull & Barnsley & Great Central Joint line in the Doncaster area, is to Great Northern pattern, with decorative barge boards and conventional locking frame windows.

N. D. Mundy

Plate 294: Small windows were a feature of Paxton signal box, on the Great Northern Railway. Note the absence of rails around the balcony This signal box, located between St Neots and Huntingdon, on the main East Coast route, was dispensed with in the mid-1960s, but until the end, remained in the green and cream livery latterly used by the LNER. The box was fitted with a 25 lever Dutton frame.

N. D. Mundy

Plate 295:   Carlton signal box, between Newark and Retford, on the Great Northern Railway. The red 'target' on the crossing gates is in two halves and is centrally sited. The gate supports are of concrete.

N. D. Mundy

Plate 296:   The brick and timber box at Newark North, with extended glazing at the south end. Note the barge boarding and the provision of four locking frame windows.

Author

Plate 297:   The latter day British Railways painting scheme defines the mouldings used in the vertically-boarded wooden box of Huntingdon North No. 1 on the East Coast Main Line. This box had a Saxby Duplex 70 lever frame.

Plate 298: The ground level brick and timber signal box, at Hainton, between Bardney and Louth, on the Great Northern Railway. Bullhead rail is used to bridge the signal wire and point rodding exit from the box.

N. D. Mundy

Plate 299: The predominantly brick signal box, at Leicester Passenger, on the Great Northern Railway. The cabin steps are of steel and post-date the box. The GNR station was also known as Leicester (Belgrave Road).

N. D. Mundy

Plate 300: A typically small Great North of Scotland Railway signal box, at Alford, the terminus of the branch from Kintore in Aberdeenshire between Aberdeen and Keith. The eaves boards are almost flush with the end boarding, which, as with the front, are not flush but slightly overlapping. No nameboard was fitted, a fairly common feature of GNSR signal boxes. When closed in BR days, all signalling was to the GNSR pattern.

W. A. C. Smith

Plate 301: Kittybrewster South signal box, lay in the fork between the main Aberdeen to Elgin line and the Waterloo Goods branch of the Great North of Scotland Railway, some two miles out of Aberdeen Joint Station. The presence of an adjacent road bridge was the main reason for its height, the lower portion, as with so many buildings in the city, being built of granite blocks.

Author

Plate 302: A larger wooden signal box, on the Great North of Scotland Railway, at Elgin West (later Elgin Centre), with projecting eaves boards for the gable roof. The Highland Railway main line passed to the rear and this box was jointly operated, controlling traffic on both GNS and HR lines.

Author

Plate 303: A hipped roof signal box, on the Aberdeen—Huntly—Inverness main line at Kennethmont.

Author

Plate 304: The large Great North of Scotland box, of all wood construction but fitted with decorative ridging to the hipped roof, at Inverurie. Connections for the main GNSR works at Inverurie were worked from this box.

Author

Plate 305: The large composite construction signal box at Aberdeen North, with wood top and concrete clad brick base. The box latterly contained a 24 lever frame after track and signalling rationalization, but after the new power box opened in 1982, at Aberdeen, this box was completely demolished.

Author

Plate 306: Stone was the construction medium for the signal box at Lossiemouth, on the branch from Elgin. The box was built of that traditional Scottish material, stone blocks, at the approaches to the goods yard.

Author

Plate 307: An end view of the signal box on the south side of the line at North Cave, 15 miles from the Hull terminus of the Hull & Barnsley Railway. The wood box was built into the side of a slight embankment and the eaves featured an inverted as well as a normal finial. Note the use of the inclined horizontal wood boarding acting as a wind break for the otherwise unprotected cabin door. Although no balcony was fitted outside the main windows, a small shelf was provided.

C. T. Goode

Plate 308: A wooden construction signal box, with a rear projection, at Wrangbrook Junction, west of Kirk Smeaton, where the main line of the Hull & Barnsley Railway from Hull (Carson Street) Station divided into three separate routes, these being to Cudworth, Wath and Denaby. The elevation of the box over rail level was dictated by the requirements for an unobstructed line of vision over the road bridge to the left of the picture. A small balcony, with a railing, was fitted outside the box at operating floor level.

C. T. Goode

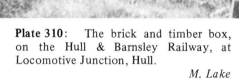

Plate 309: The wooden signal box, platform-mounted, situated at Sprotborough, between Mexborough and Kirk Smeaton, on the Hull & Barnsley Railway. Note the small oil lamp on the front elevation.

C. T. Goode

Plate 310: The brick and timber box, on the Hull & Barnsley Railway, at Locomotive Junction, Hull.

M. Lake

Plate 311: The brick and timber platform signal box, at Kirk Smeaton, situated some 41 miles to the west of Hull, on the Hull & Barnsley Railway main line.

C. T. Goode

Plate 312: The small wooden signal box at Penicuik, on the North British Railway. Sparse use, latterly, of the frame led to window shutters being provided against vandalism.

Author

Plate 313: The vertical-timbered box at Lumphinnans Central Junction, Fife. The area was heavily undermined by colliery workings.

Author

Plate 314: The wooden signal box, at Kingsbarns, on the East of Fife Railway, between Crail and St. Andrews. A typical North British tablet platform, with oil lamp, is shown to the left of the box. Note the unusual glazing below the main windows.

Author

Plate 315: The partially dismantled signal box at Commonhead, near Airdrie, gives a good example of framing used in standard NBR brick and timber boxes.

Plate 316: An elevated Stevens ground frame was housed in this small brick and timber box at Cairntows, Edinburgh. **(See Plate 138)**.

Author

Plate 317: Jedburgh signal box, the branch terminal, retained many North British hallmarks, such as tablet platform and finials, well into the British Railways era.

J. E. Hay

Plate 318: This brick structure at Warriston Junction, Edinburgh controlled a small yard at one time, but was later adapted for staff accommodation. Note the space for non-existent locking at ground level.

Author

Plate 319: The platform-mounted brick signal box at Largo on the East of Fife line from Thornton to Crail.

Author

Plate 320: An older brick box at Dumbuck, between Bowling and Dumbarton, which was closed in 1961 when the portion of line was abandoned after electrification. Note the pure North British Railway Stevens ground signals, crossing gates supports of iron and high curves of the cabin windows facing the running line.

W. A. C. Smith

Plate 321: A brick base with enlarged glazing area was incorporated in Dysart box, north of Kirkcaldy.

Author

Plate 322: The brick box with wood extension for level crossing control, at Bonnyrigg, on the Peebles line. Note the different crossing gates and iron supports, and the absence of red gate 'targets'.

Author

Plate 323: Musselburgh box was originally of brick construction, but extended by wood, the operating floor glazing being altered at the time. The station was the terminus of the North British branch, which left the East Coast Main Line at Inveresk Junction, 6½ miles out from Edinburgh Waverley.

J. E. Hay

Plate 324: The small North British Railway signal box at Thornton South Junction, in Fife, with wood panelling over the windows reducing the glazing height. The box was on the main Edinburgh to Aberdeen line and also controlled freight diverging lines into the Fife coalfields in the area.

Author

Plate 325: Riccarton South signal box was of concrete-faced brick construction and lay in the fork between the Hexham and Carlisle lines. The signalman's house was to the rear of the box.

Author

Plate 326: The tall four storey box, situated at Carlisle Canal Junction, in the fork of the Silloth branch. This box also served the main North British Railway locomotive shed at Carlisle Canal, together with the main Carlisle–Hawick–Edinburgh, the 'Waverley Route'. A verandah ran round the glazing and facilitated cleaning.

Author

Plate 327: The dressed stone frontage of Kielder Forest signal box was typical of many cabins situated on the Border Counties' lines.

H. C. Casserley

Plate 328: Hardengreen Junction signal box was a tall brick structure but with a wooden overhang. Operating floor level access was partially outside and partially inside. Note the tablet platform for diverging trains using the Peebles line.

R. Montgomery

Plate 329: Innerleithen signal box was sited in a restricted space area and consequently had a double overhang. Note the decorative wood valancing at the base of the projection. The lower steps were a later modification and tablet exchange facilities were incorporated.

Author

Plate 330: Much modified was a signal box at Heriot on the Edinburgh to Carlisle main line.

Author

Plate 331: The most westerly signal box on the British mainland was at Arisaig on the North British West Highland extension line. The box was to a basic Railway Signal Company pattern, the end nameboards being of London & North Eastern type, with that on the front being an original.

Author

Plate 332: West Highland line boxes were generally different from others on the North British Railway. Depicted here is Glen Douglas box, which was finished in concrete over a brick base. As at Riccarton, staff accommodation was to the rear.

Author

Plate 333: Corrour, further north, still sports the original enamelled West Highland nameplate on the signalman's house in the foreground. Station buildings and platforms are to the rear in this photograph.

Author

Plate 334: The platform-mounted signal box at Tulloch, one of the few West Highland stations with separate 'up' and 'down' platforms, most being of the island type.

Author

Plate 335: The completely wooden platform-mounted box, at Crail, built of 'tongue and groove' vertical boarding.
Author

Plate 336: The subterraneous location of Charing Cross signal box resulted in a facing of white tiles. The station nameboard also sufficed for the cabin.
Author

Plate 337: Wemyss Castle signal box was integral with the station buildings, with an appropriate projection for maximum visibility. The station was on the Thornton to Methil (North British) line.
Author

Plate 338: Velvet Hall signal box, of all wood construction, was on the North Eastern line which made an end-on connection with the North British Railway at Sprouston (Mellingdean Junction), en route to Kelso.

J. E. Hay

Plate 339: Little Mill signal box, also in Northumberland, was on the East Coast Main Line and was situated between Berwick-upon-Tweed and Alnmouth.

Author

Plate 340: Mindrum signal box on the Coldstream to Alnwick line incorporated the box in the main station buildings and is the extension into the platform seen in the centre of the picture. Framing was wooden, surrounded in the same style as the station waiting-rooms.

J. E. Hay

Plate 341: The wooden, gantry-mounted, signal box at Hexham, on the Newcastle to Carlisle line. This style of box was used in several locations by the North Eastern Railway, where space or sighting restrictions precluded the use of a more conventional lineside structure.

Author

Plate 342: Grosmont signal box, on the Darlington to Whitby line, was built mainly of wood on a brick base, with all four sides overhanging the base. Pictured in the fork of the Whitby to Middlesbrough/Pickering line, it was moved to a new site in 1979 by the North York Moors Railway Trust.

Author

Plate 343: Grosmont Crossing box was a small wooden structure to the left of the gates on the Whitby to Pickering line.
Author

Plate 344: Glaisdale signal box, on the Whitby and Battersby line, is an all brick structure which was not platform-mounted, a wooden 'bridge' being provided over the point and wire runs.

Author

Plate 345: Guisborough Junction had a hipped roof box with a slatted end at the apex, and was located to the east of Middlesbrough. Being in a fork, the box is double sided.

Author

Plate 346: North Ormesby signal box, with its attractive barge boards, lost much of its roof section by the intrusion of the footbridge.

R. Preston

Plate 347: Harrogate South box is of all wood 'lean to' construction.

R. Preston

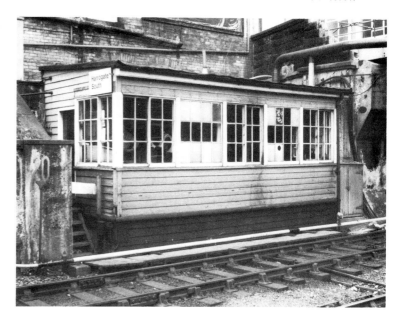

Plate 348: Wolsingham box, between Darlington and Stanhope, was a brick and timber 'lean to', the rear wall of which was the wall of the cutting. Note the small spectacled North Eastern Railway lower quadrant signal in the foreground.

R. Montgomery

Plate 349: Long outside steps and overhanging wooden operating floor were featured at Bishop Auckland North box.

R. Montgomery

Plate 350: The last surviving signal box at Bishop Auckland was that at East Junction, which was of conventional North Eastern Railway outline and was of brick and timber construction.

Author

Plate 351: Ponteland signal box, an all wood type, was on the branch from South Gosforth to Benton, near Newcastle upon Tyne. Note the roof ventilation cowling on the roof ridge and the North Eastern Railway pattern signals at the platform end.

J. Johnston

Plate 352: North of Darlington, the Stockton & Darlington line crossed the East Coast Main Line on the level. In the south-east angle of the junction was the small signal box known as 'S & D Crossing'.

E. Haigh Collection

Plate 353: At Selby, the East Coast Main Line was intersected by a river. The North Eastern Region box, in the foreground, controlled the station area and the elevated box, to the rear, controlled the swing bridge. Electrical services were maintained to the latter by an overhead cable, the box turning with the bridge.

Author

Plate 354: A view of Selby Swing Bridge cabin and bridge showing the connecting cable. In this illustration, the bridge is open for river traffic and a small coaster is 'crossing' the East Coast Main Line.

Author

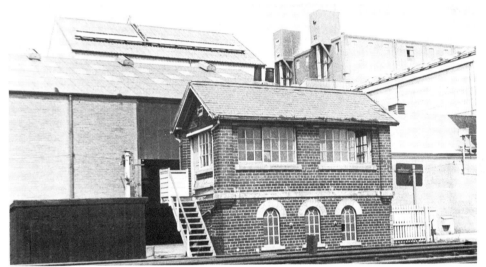

Plate 355: Barlby, between York and Selby, was one of the southernmost N E R boxes and is in the style of North Eastern brick boxes, the tops of the locking frame windows being rounded.

N. D. Mundy

Plate 356: Heck box has less ornate windows and was on the Selby to York line and on closure as a block post, was adapted for other railway use.

N. D. Mundy

Plate 357: Crabley Creek signal box was on the Hull to Goole line of the North Eastern Railway, the original wooden steps being replaced by the more modern steel type.

N. D. Mundy

Plate 358: Seamer had old and new types of North Eastern signal boxes adjacent, the brick and timber building undertaking the work of the displaced brick type box.

H. G. Wilson

Plate 359: The brick and timber North Eastern box, at Melton Lane, with the operating floor glazing extending to 'cant rail' level.

N. D. Mundy

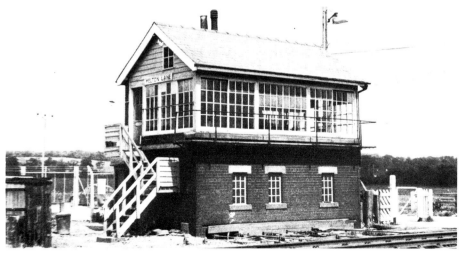

Plate 360: Ferriby signal box, situated on the Hull to Selby line, was platform-mounted and of brick and timber construction. Locking frame windows have been bricked in.

Author

Plate 361: The large double sided North Eastern box, at Hull West Parade, featuring a side ducket for improved vision. Locking frame windows have been bricked in.

Author

Plate 362: The octagonal box at Anlaby Road, Hull, with its attractive roof valancing.

C. T. Goode

Plate 363: Ganton signal box, on the Malton to Scarborough line, is of standard NER brick construction but is fitted with a wooden projection for level crossing control visibility.

H. G. Wilson

Plate 364: The double level crossing gates and controlling signal box at Newton Kyme, on the Harrogate to Church Fenton (NER) line. Gate supports are timber baulks and the left hand lamp has shrouded glazing to avoid conflict with signal aspects. A sleeper walkway connects the platform ramps.

LNER

Plate 365: Milford South is a large North Eastern wooden box with large glazed locking frame windows. Note the abbreviation of the nameboard. All except one of the signal arms are of North Eastern ancestry.

LNER

Appendix One

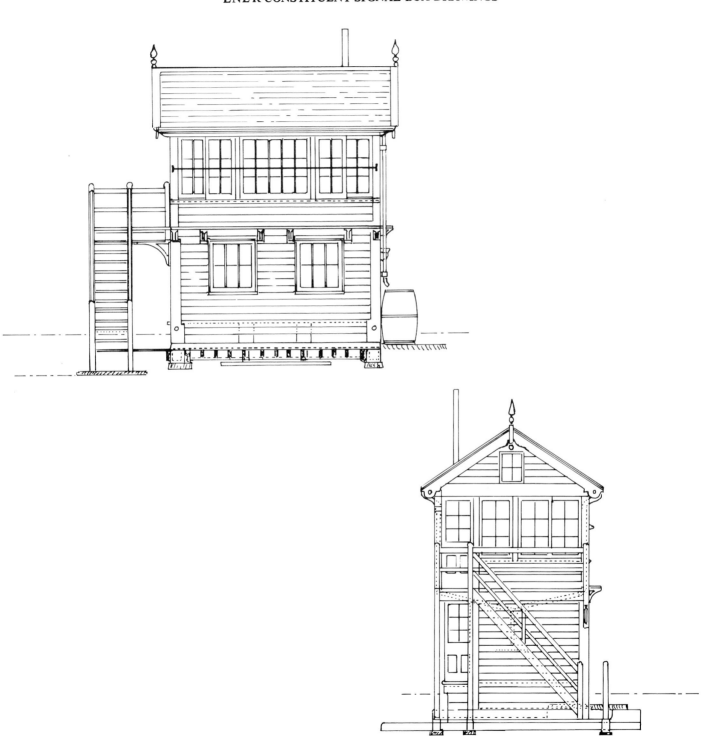

Figure 89: A typical wooden signal box (Great Central Railway).

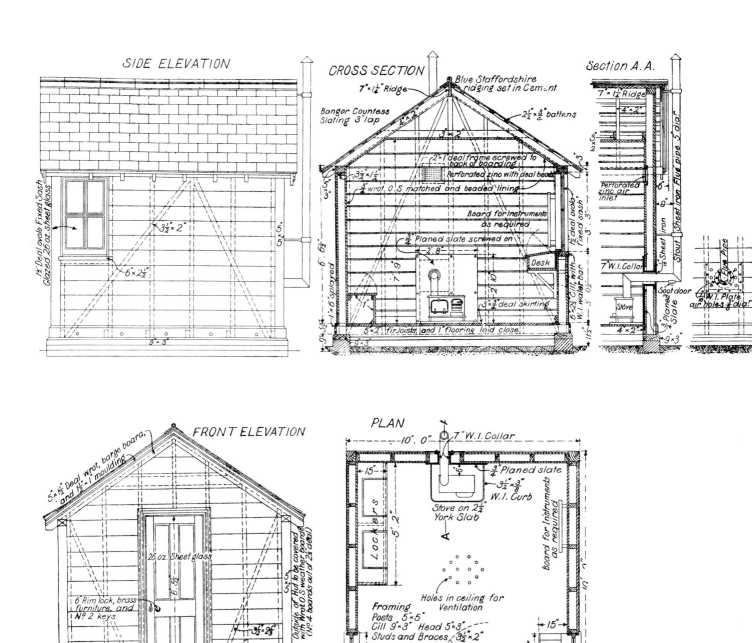

Figure 90: A standard design for a signal hut at block stations (Great Eastern Railway).

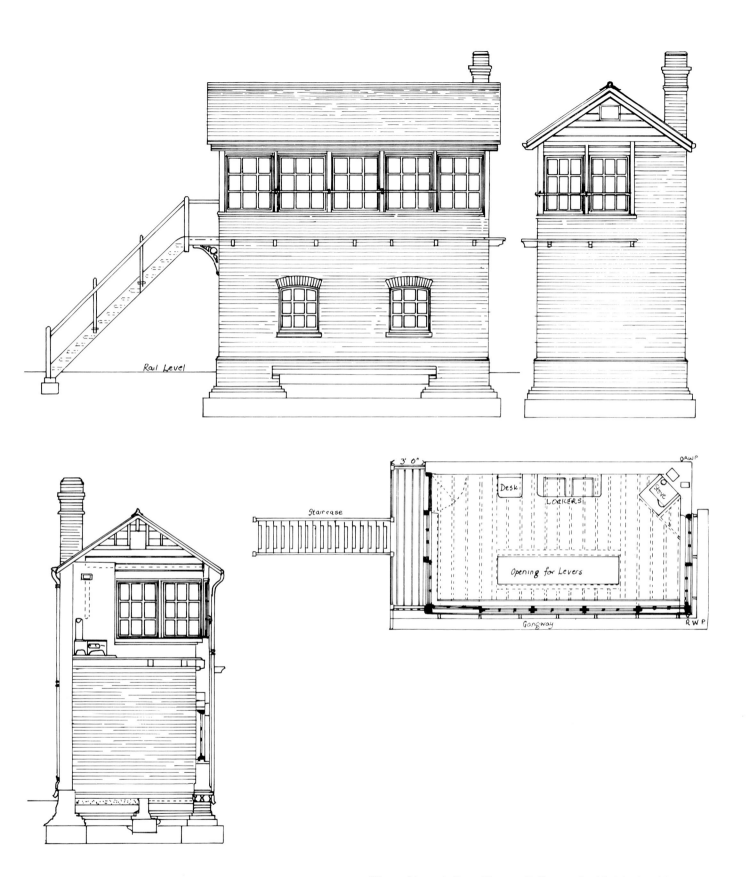

Figure 91:   A Great Eastern Railway raised brick signal box.

Rail Level

Staircase

3' 0"

Desk

LOCKERS

Stove

Opening for Levers

Gangway

RWP

RWP

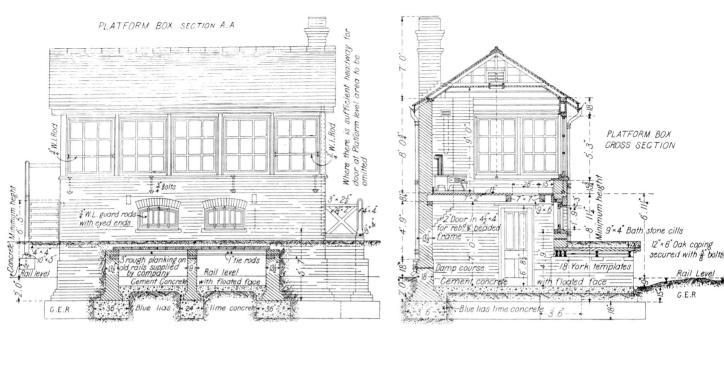

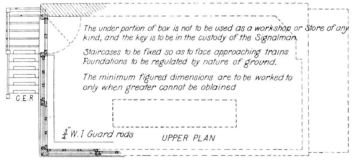

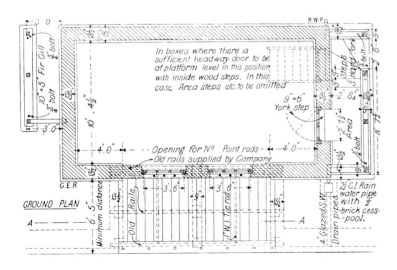

Figure 92: A standard design for a platform brick signal box (Great Eastern Railway).

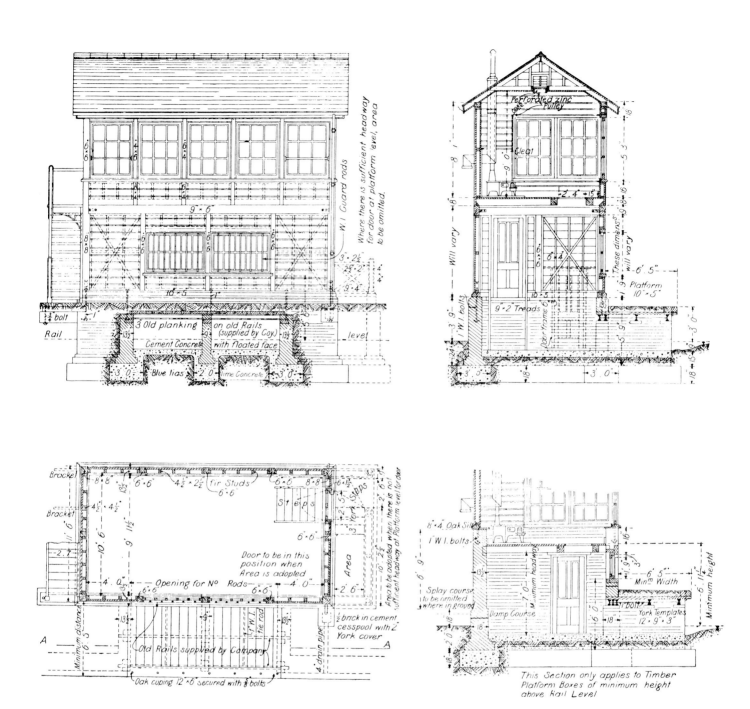

Figure 93: A wooden platform mounted signal box (Great Eastern Railway).

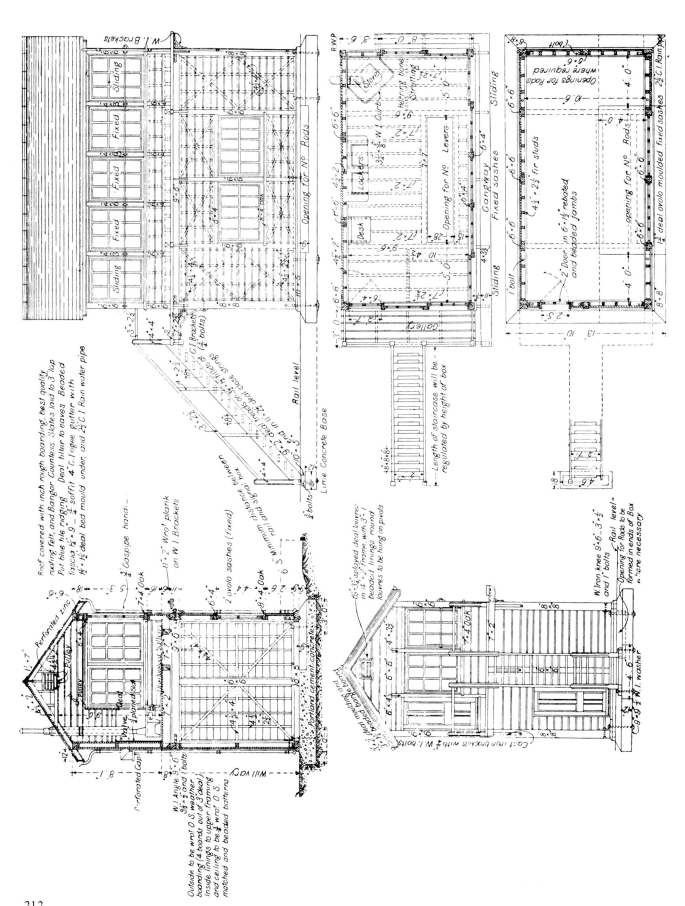

Figure 94: The standard design for a raised wood signal box (Great Eastern Railway).

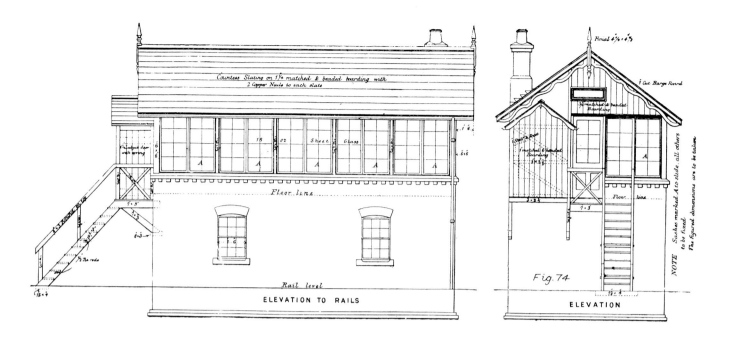

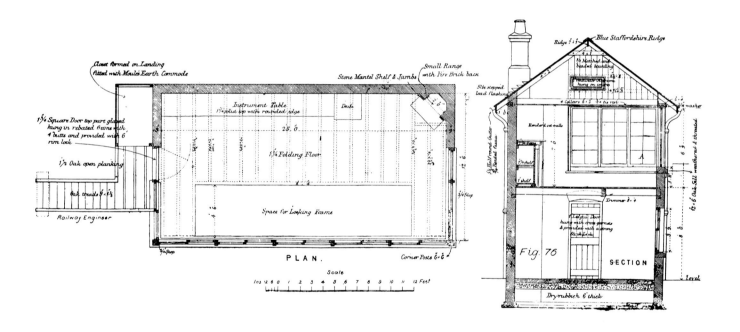

Figure 95: A brick signal cabin (Great Northern Railway).

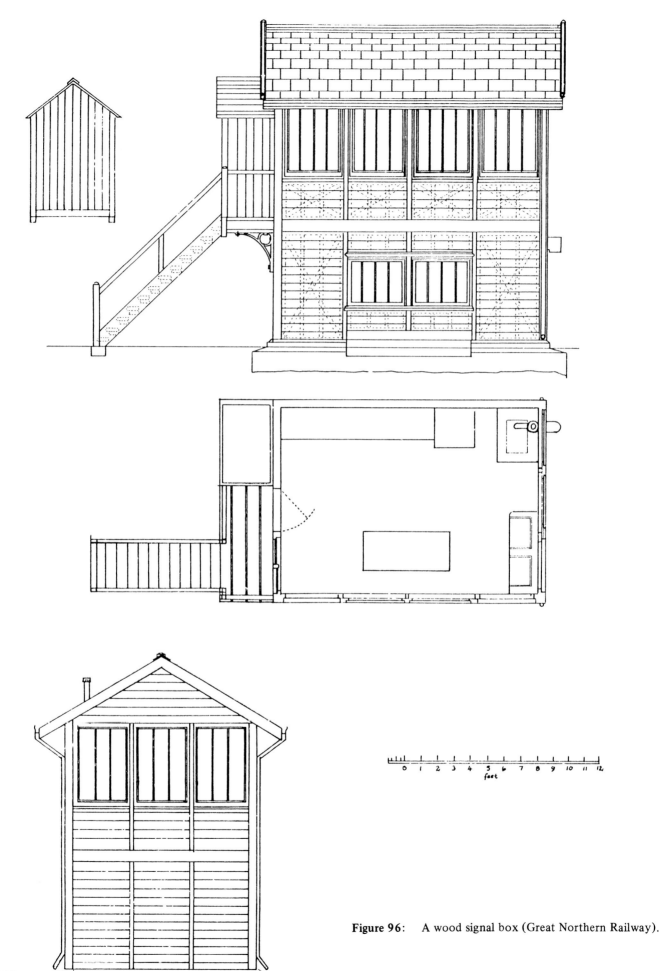

Figure 96:   A wood signal box (Great Northern Railway).

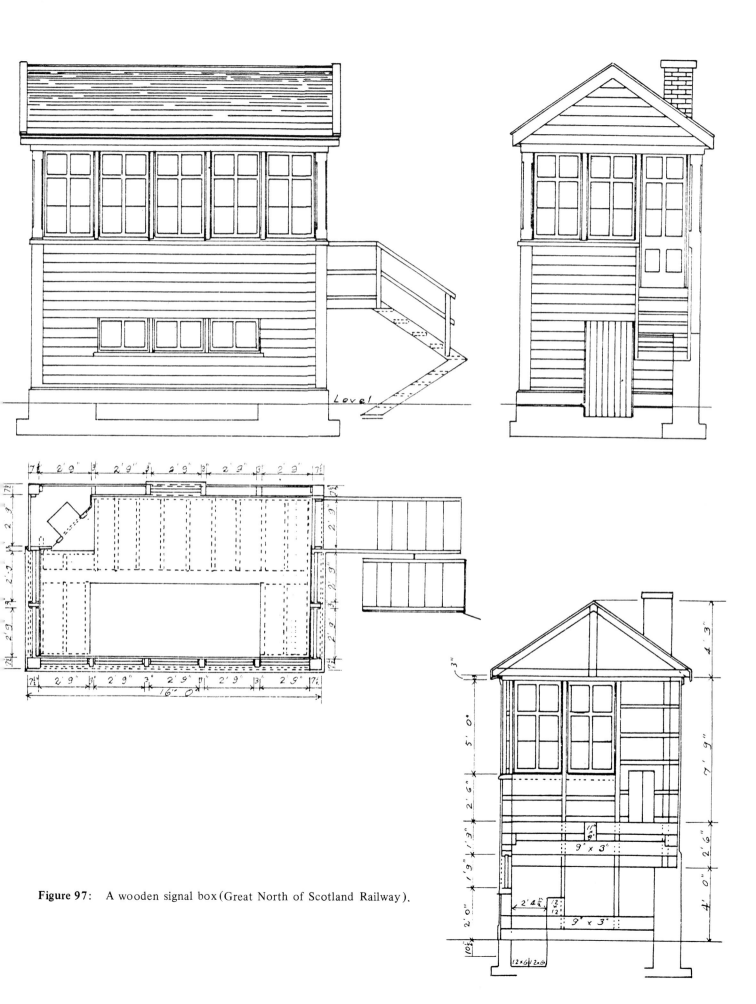

Figure 97: A wooden signal box (Great North of Scotland Railway).

Front   End

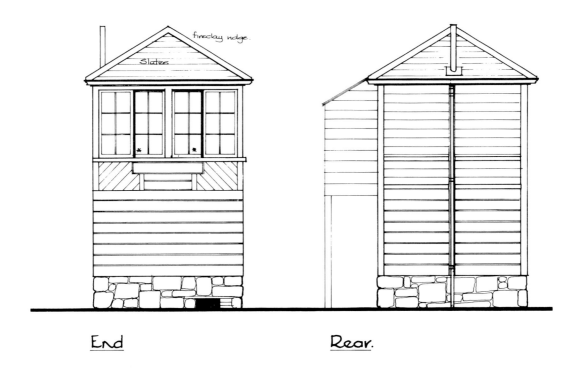

End   Rear.

A small wooden signal box (North Eastern Railway).

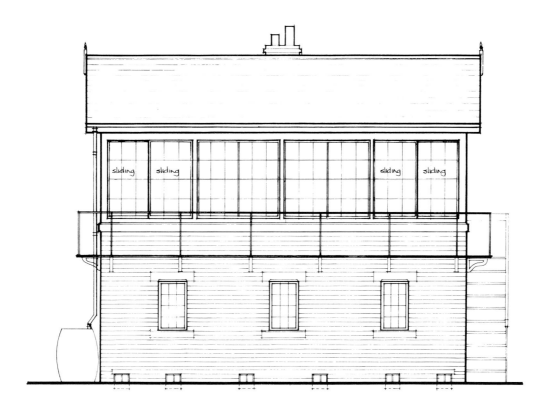

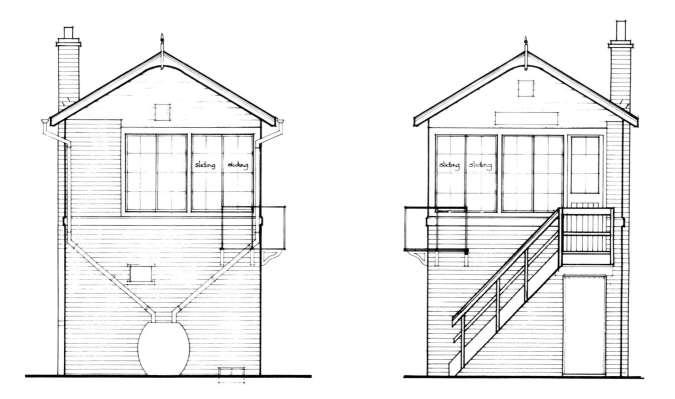

Figure 99: A standard design for a brick signal box (North Eastern Railway).

217

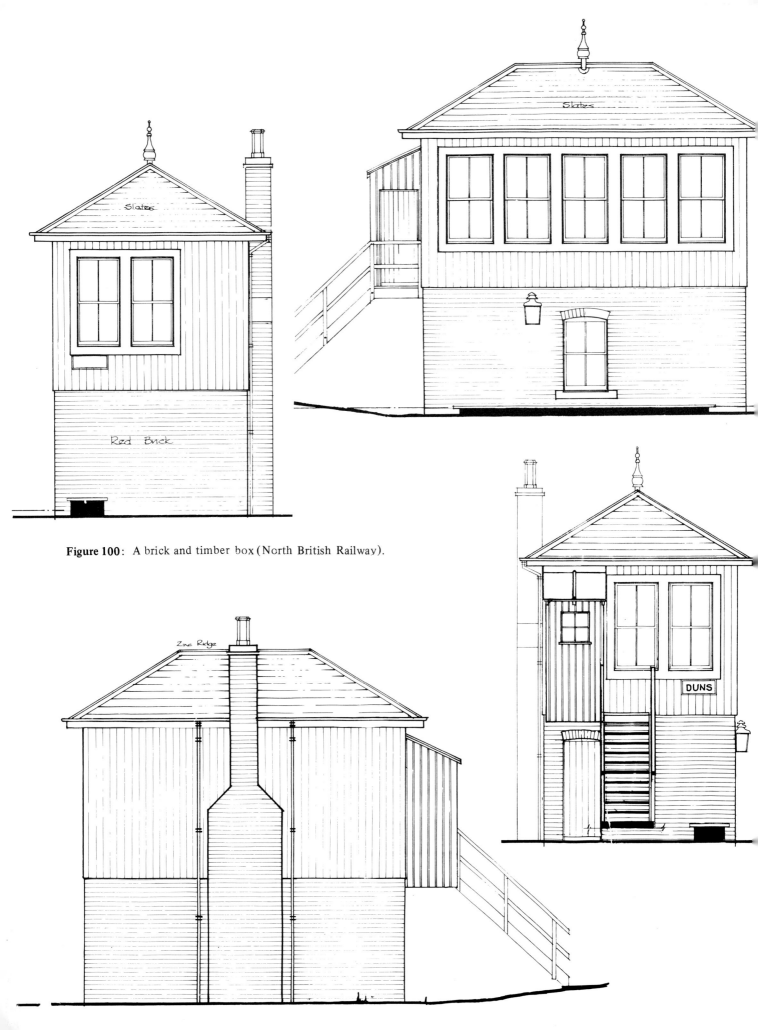

Slates

Slates

Red Brick

Figure 100: A brick and timber box (North British Railway).

Zinc Ridge

DUNS

Appendix Two

SIGNAL BOX LEVER FRAME VARIATIONS – GNR

Signal Box	Equipment	No. of Levers
Belle Isle 'up'	Saxby Duplex	45
Copenhagen Junction	Saxby Duplex	50
Goods & Mineral Junction	Railway Signal Company	100
Five Arch Bridge	McKenzie & Holland 4 inch	30
Holloway South 'down'	Railway Signal Company	50
Holloway South 'up'	Saxby Duplex	40
Holloway North 'down'	McKenzie & Holland 4 inch	30
Holloway North 'up'	Dutton	80
Holloway Carriage Sidings	Dutton	25
Ashburton Grove	Dutton	20
East Goods	McKenzie & Holland 5 inch	
Finsbury Park No. 1	Saxby Duplex	60
Finsbury Park No. 2	Dutton	70
Finsbury Park No. 3	McKenzie & Holland 4 inch	80
Finsbury Park No. 4	Dutton	60
Finsbury Park No. 5	McKenzie & Holland 4 inch	60
Finsbury Park No. 6	McKenzie & Holland 4 inch	60
Finsbury Park No. 7	McKenzie & Holland Rocker Shaft	18
Harringay 'up'	Saxby Duplex	25
Harringay 'down'	McKenzie & Holland Cam & Tappet	30
Harringay Sidings	McKenzie & Holland Rocker Shaft	5
Harringay 'up' Goods	McKenzie & Holland Cam & Tappet	80
Hornsey 'up'	Saxby Duplex	35
Hornsey 'down'	Evans & O'Donnell	30
Hornsey 'up' Goods	McKenzie & Holland Cam & Tappet	80
Wood Green No. 1	Saxby Duplex	60
Wood Green No. 2	Saxby Duplex	40
Wood Green No. 3	Saxby Duplex	40
Wood Green No. 4	Saxby & Farmer Rocker	60
Wood Green Tunnel	Saxby & Farmer Rocker	25
New Southgate	McKenzie & Holland 4 inch	70
Cemetery	McKenzie & Holland 4 inch	25
Oakley Park	McKenzie & Holland 4 inch	40
New Barnet South	Saxby Duplex	60
New Barnet North	McKenzie & Holland 4 inch	65
Greenwood	Saxby Duplex	25
Hadley Wood	Great Northern Railway	12
Potters Bar	Great Northern Railway of Ireland	65
Marsh More	Saxby & Farmer Rocker	25
Red Hall	Great Northern Railway	25
Hatfield No. 1	Saxby & Farmer Rocker	70
Hatfield No. 2	Railway Signal Company	80
Hatfield No. 3	Railway Signal Company	80
Hatfield No. 4	Saxby & Farmer Rocker	60
Welwyn Garden City	Saxby Duplex	80 + 20
Welwyn North	Railway Signal Company	40
Woolmer Green 7	Saxby Duplex	25
Knebworth	Saxby & Farmer Rocker	70
Langley	Railway Signal Company	40
Stevenage South	Saxby & Farmer Rocker	45
Stevenage North	Saxby Duplex	
Hitchin South	Railway Signal Company	55
Hitchin Yard	Stevens	45
Cambridge Junction	McKenzie & Holland 5 inch	72
Cadwell	Evans & O'Donnell	25
Three Counties	Saxby Duplex	65
Arlesley	Dutton	72
Langford	Dutton	45
Biggleswade South	Railway Signal Company	45
Biggleswade North	Railway Signal Company	40
Sandy	Saxby Duplex	80
Sandy Junction	McKenzie & Holland	18
Everton	Saxby Duplex	25
Tempsford	Dutton	70
St. Neots	Saxby Duplex	55
Paxton	Dutton	25
Offord	Dutton	60
Ouse Bridge	McKenzie & Holland	18
Huntingdon No. 1	Saxby Duplex	70
Huntingdon No. 2	Saxby Duplex	65
Stukeley	Dutton	20
Abbots Ripton	McKenzie & Holland	40

Signal Box	Equipment	No. of Levers
Connington South	Dutton	25
Connington North	Dutton	20
Holme	Saxby & Farmer Rocker 4 inch and 5 inch	65
Yaxley	Railway Signal Company	45
Fletton	Railway Signal Company	40
Crescent Junction	McKenzie & Holland	70
Bounds Green	McKenzie & Holland	30
Bows Park	McKenzie & Holland	20
Palmers Green	McKenzie & Holland	20
Winchmore Green	Saxby & Farmer Ground Frame	8
Grange Park	Saxby Duplex, Atkinson Pattern	25
Enfield Chase	Saxby Duplex, Atkinson Pattern	25
Gordon Hill	Saxby Duplex, FAA & Co.	30
Crews Hill	Saxby Duplex	25
Cuffley	Saxby Duplex	25
Bayford	Saxby Ground Frame	8
Hertford North	Saxby Duplex	65
Stapleford	Saxby Ground Frame	8
Watton	Saxby Ground Frame	8
Letchworth	McKenzie & Holland	35
Baldock	Stevens	31
Ashwell	Saxby & Farmer Rocker	25
Litlington Crossing	Saxby Spiral Spindle	5
Royston	Saxby & Farmer Rocker	35
Meldreth	Saxby & Famrer Rocker	30
Shepreth Road Crossing	Saxby Spiral Spindle	5
Shepreth	Saxby & Farmer Rocker	30
Foxton	Saxby Duplex	30
Harston	Saxby & Farmer Rocker	30
Hauxton	Saxby Spiral Spindle	5
Ayot	Saxby Duplex	25
Wheathamstead	Saxby Duplex	20
Harpenden	McKenzie & Holland 6 inch	30
Luton Hoo	Saxby Duplex	20
Luton East	Saxby Duplex	35
Luton Yard	Saxby Duplex	40
Luton West	Great Northern Railway	30
Chaul End	Great Northern Railway	10
Dunstable	LNWR Pattern	25
Nortons	Great Northern Railway Ground Frame	2
English Electric	Saxby Ground Frame	2
Attimore Hall	Saxby Ground Frame	3
Birch Hall Tip	Great Northern Railway Ground Frame	2
Cole Green	Saxby Duplex	25
Hertingfordbury Station	Great Northern Railway Ground Frame	2
Hertingfordbury Sidings	Great Northern Railway Ground Frame	2
Webbs Siding	Great Northern Railway Ground Frame	2
Hertford Goods		
Porthill Bridge	Saxby Ground Frame	6
Good Shead	Saxby Ground Frame	4
Harham	Saxby Ground Frame	3
Widewater	Saxby Ground Frame	3
Dorkermill Crossing	Saxby Ground Frame	4
Smarts	Saxby Ground Frame	2
Sadlers	Saxby Ground Frame	2
Gasworks	Saxby Ground Frame	2
Godmanchester	McKenzie & Holland 5 inch	45
Gasworks Crossing	Saxby Ground Frame	3
Huntingdon No. 1	Saxby Duplex	70
Buckden	Midland Tumbler	8
Grafham	Midland Tumbler	10
Longstow	Midland Tumbler	10
Kimbolton	Midland Tumbler	30
Raunds	Midland Tumbler	20